CONTENTS

Published by Pedigree Books Limited
Beech Hill House, Walnut Gardens
Exeter, Devon EX4 4DH
Email: books@pedigreegroup.co.uk
Published 2007

TIMELINE

-5,000,0000,000	GALAXY FORMS
-35,000	BIRTH OF THE RAKATA EMPIRE
-27,500	ALDERAAN COLONIZED
-25,200	FALL OF THE RAKATA EMPIRE
-25,100	TREATY OF VONTOR
-25,100	CORELLIANS AND DUROS INTRODUCED TO HYPERSPACE
-25,000	PERLEMIAN TRADE ROUTE
-25,000	CORELLIAN RUN ESTABLISHED
-25,000	DUROS COLONIZE NEIMOIDIA
-25,000	1ST GALACTIC REPUBLIC FORMED
-25,000	CREATION OF THE JEDI ORDER
-17,000	FIRST ALSAKAN CRISIS
-8000	REPUBLIC OUTPOST ON MALASTARE
-7000	HUNDRED-YEAR DARKNESS
-5500	RIMMA TRADE ROUTE ORIGIN
-5000	UNIFICATION WARS END
-5000	GREAT HYPERSPACE WAR
-5000	FALL OF THE SITH EMPIRE
-4250	VULTAR CATACLYSM
<-4000	GANK MASSACRE
-4015	GREAT DROID REVOLUTION
-4000	BATTLE OF BASILISK
-4000	BEAST WARS OF ONDERON
-3998	FREEDON NADD UPRISING
-3996	THE GREAT SITH WAR
-3995	MANDALORIAN WARS BEGIN
-3986	ULIC QEL-DROMA'S REDEMPTION
-3964	THE HUNT FOR ZAYNE CARRICK
-3961	JEDI CIVIL WAR
-3956	MALAK WAR (RETURN OF REVAN)
-3951	RETURN OF THE EXILE
-3900	NABOO COLONIZED
-3000	HYDIAN WAY ROUTE BLAZED
-2000	NEW SITH WARS BEGIN
-1003	RISE OF DARTH BANE
-1000	BATTLE OF RUUSAN
-1000	SITH GO INTO HIDING
-896	YODA BORN
~-600	JABBA THE HUTT BORN
-490	CORPORATE SECTOR FORMED
-350	TRADE FEDERATION ESTABLISHED
-340	CHU'UNTHOR CRASHES ON DATHOMIR
-200	CHEWBACCA BORN
-102	COUNT DOOKU BORN
-92	QUI-GON BORN
-57	OBI-WAN BORN
-50	ARKANIAN REVOLUTION
-46	AMIDALA BORN
-46	VERUNA BECOMES KING
-44	OBI-WAN BECOMES QUI-GON'S PADAWAN
-44	STARK HYPERSPACE WAR
-41.9	ANAKIN BORN
-37	MISSION TO ORD MANTELL
-32.5	ERIADU TRADE SUMMIT
-32.5	AMIDALA ELECTED QUEEN
-32.5	MAUL INFILTRATES BLACK SUN
-32	THE PHANTOM MENACE
-32	BATTLE OF NABOO
-32	PALPATINE ELECTED CHANCELLOR
-32	COUNT DOOKU LEAVES THE JEDI ORDER
-32	JANGO FETT CHOSEN TO BE CLONE HOST
-31	DEATH OF SHARAD HETT
-29	MISSION TO ZONAMA SEKOT
-29	HAN SOLO BORN
-28	ANAKIN BUILDS HIS LIGHTSABER
-27	OUTBOUND FLIGHT

-22.1	ANSION THREATENS TO SECEDE	0	EMPEROR DISSOLVES SENATE
-22	ATTACK OF THE CLONES	0	LUKE MEETS HAN SOLO
-22	BATTLE OF GEONOSIS	0	DESTRUCTION OF ALDERAAN
-22	CLONE WARS BEGIN	0	OBI-WAN BECOMES ONE WITH THE FORCE
-22	MARRIAGE OF ANAKIN AND PADMÉ	0	HEROES ESCAPE DEATH STAR
-21.5	BATTLE OF MUUNILINST	0	BATTLE OF YAVIN
-21.5	BATTLE OF HYPORI	0	DEATH OF GRAND MOFF TARKIN
-21	BATTLE OF JABIIM	0	DESTRUCTION OF THE DEATH STAR
-19.5	YODA CONFRONTS DOOKU ON VJUN	0	WALEX BLISSEX JOINS THE ALLIANCE
-19.5	ANAKIN BECOMES A JEDI KNIGHT	0	A-WING DESIGNED
-19.5	OUTER RIM SIEGES BEGIN	0.5	LUKE SKYWALKER DISCOVERS HOTH
-19.1	JEDI HUNT FOR DARTH SIDIOUS	0.5	ALLIANCE FLEES YAVIN
-19	REVENGE OF THE SITH	0.5	DODONNA CAPTURED
-19	BATTLE OF CORUSCANT	1	CRIX MADINE DEFECTS TO ALLIANCE
-19	DEATH OF MACE WINDU	1	B-WING DESIGNED
-19	ANAKIN BECOMES DARTH VADER	2	CIRCARPOUS JOINS ALLIANCE
-19	ORDER SIXTY-SIX	2	ALLIANCE BUILDS BASE ON HOTH
-19	PALPATINE DECLARES HIMSELF EMPEROR	3	THE EMPIRE STRIKES BACK
-19	VADER/OBI-WAN DUEL ON MUSTAFAR	3	BATTLE OF HOTH
		3	LUKE TRAINS ON DAGOBAH
-19	LUKE & LEIA BORN	3	HAN SOLO FROZEN IN CARBONITE
-19	DEATH OF PADMÉ AMIDALA	3	LUKE DUELS VADER ON CLOUD CITY
-18	EYE OF PALPATINE	3.5	BLACK SUN PLOT TO KILL LUKE
-7	DISASTER ON FALLEEN	3.5	BOBA FETT DELIVERS SOLO TO JABBA
-4	LANDO CALRISSIAN'S ADVENTURES	3.5	DEATH OF PRINCE XIZOR
-2	LANDO LOSES THE FALCON TO HAN	4	RETURN OF THE JEDI
-2	CHEWIE MARRIES MALLA	4	BOBA FETT FALLS INTO THE SARLACC
-2	CORELLIAN TREATY	4	DEATH OF JABBA THE HUTT
-1	SEARCH FOR THE YAVIN VASSILIKA	4	DEATH OF YODA
0	ALLIANCE STEALS DEATH STAR PLANS	4	BATTLE OF ENDOR
0	A NEW HOPE	4	DEATH OF THE EMPEROR
0	PRINCESS LEIA CAPTURED	4	REDEMPTION/DEATH OF ANAKIN SKYWALKER
0	LUKE MEETS R2-D2 AND C-3PO	4	DESTRUCTION OF DEATH STAR II
0	OBI-WAN SHOWS LUKE THE FORCE		

THE JEDI ORDER

For each Jedi, training began in infancy. All connection to previous family life was lost. At this stage, a single Master would instruct clan groups of Jedi hopefuls, who were called younglings.

IDENTITY FILE

The ancient Jedi Order was a noble group of protectors, brought together by their belief in and observance of the Force. The Order stemmed from a more civilized, classical time in galactic history, and it spanned over 1000 generations.

The Jedi trained, studied and planned from the Jedi Temple on Coruscant. Its beautiful towers rose high above the surrounding structures on the city planet. They were governed by the High Council, which consisted of 12 Jedi. Most of those were Jedi Masters, and they contemplated the very nature of the Force. They were the main interface between the Jedi and the government of the Republic.

EARLY HISTORY

The origins of the Jedi Order have been lost, but much of their early history has been recorded in special information modules called Jedi Holocrons. These Holocrons can only be activated by those who are strong in the Force, and it requires a trained Jedi to successfully navigate through the layers of information. From the few Holocrons that remain, some scholars believe that the Jedi order began on the ancient world of Ossus.

Throughout the millennia, the Jedi Code has evolved and changed to remain relevant to the galaxy around it. For instance, while it now dictates that a Jedi Master may only have one Padawan at a time, in the ancient past, it was not always so. Revered masters, like Arca Jeth of Arkania, had several students.

TO BECOME A JEDI

To become a Jedi requires the deepest commitment and most serious mind. It is not a challenge to be undertaken lightly. Jedi training is rigidly structured and codified to enforce discipline. Jedi candidates are detected, identified and taken into the Order as infants. One method of detection is through blood sampling. Those with great Force potential often have high midi-chlorian counts in their bloodstream.

As the Jedi mature, an apprentice is paired with a single Master to continue the next phase of the training. According to the Jedi Code, a Jedi Master may only have one Padawan at a time. Near the end of training, each Padawan must undergo a number of trials before earning the rank of Knight.

The next significant level of rank in the Jedi order is the Jedi Master. This rank is reserved for those who have shown exceptional devotion and skill in the Force.

THE FORCE

The Force is a mystical energy field that is created by and a part of all living things. Through their connection to the living Force, the Jedi can wield great power and attain deep wisdom. In training, younglings wear helmets to block their vision, which aids them in using the Force to see, rather than using their physical senses.

THE JEDI CODE

THERE IS NO EMOTION;
THERE IS PEACE.

THERE IS NO IGNORANCE;
THERE IS KNOWLEDGE.

THERE IS NO PASSION;
THERE IS SERENITY.

THERE IS NO DEATH;
THERE IS THE FORCE.

THE LOST TWENTY

Only 20 Jedi have ever voluntarily renounced their commissions. They are known as the Lost Twenty. A Jedi who fails in his training can be a very serious threat. The dark side of the Force is deeply alluring to the impatient, and students have been lured to its call with devastating consequences.

"FOR OVER A THOUSAND GENERATIONS THE JEDI KNIGHTS WERE THE GUARDIANS OF PEACE AND JUSTICE IN THE OLD REPUBLIC."

APPEARANCE

The Jedi dress in simple robes and carry specialised field gear for their missions. While training, a Padawan wears his or her hair short, with a long braid to indicate their status. When they have achieved the rank of Knight, they grow their hair long. Their weapon, the lightsaber, is both elegant and deadly when in the hands of a trained master.

As the Galactic Republic grew and flourished over the centuries, the Jedi served it faithfully, maintaining law and order through their peaceful connection to the Force.

THE JEDI IN HIDING

Overnight, everything changed. The Jedi were branded as enemies of the state. Palpatine's new Sith apprentice, Darth Vader, destroyed the Jedi Temple and killed the younglings who lived there. As the new Empire came to power, the Jedi were almost extinct. The only survivors of the once great Order, Obi-Wan Kenobi and the Jedi Master Yoda, were forced into hiding. They could only hope that the day would come when the Jedi would return again.

SWORN ENEMIES

The order of the Sith is eternally bent on domination through subservience to the Force's dark side. Founded by former Jedi, the Sith turned their back on the pursuit of knowledge and peace. Instead, they greedily sought strength and power through the Force's negative energies.

The Jedi destroyed the Sith and believed that the order was no more. However, this was a dangerous and blinkered belief. The Sith continued to exist in secret, concealing their intentions under a guise of friendship, waiting only for the day when they could seize power and destroy the Jedi ranks.

DARK TIMES

The sudden appearance of a Sith Lord during the Battle of Naboo alarmed the Jedi Council, but they disposed of the threat. However, according to Sith lore, the Sith always travelled in pairs - a Master and an Apprentice. For a decade, there was no physical sign of the remaining Sith villain, but evidence of his power began to appear.

The Jedi Order's ability to use the Force inexplicably began to weaken. A Separatist movement increased disturbance and violence throughout the galaxy, and the Jedi were overburdened and overstretched. In trying to maintain the peace, many Jedi fell. By the time that the first shots of the Clone Wars were fired, a mere 200 Jedi were readily available for the conflict.

The Clone Wars tested the Jedi and pushed them to breaking point. They were forced to transform from an order of peacekeepers to one of military commanders, serving as battlefield generals for the Republic's new clone army. They were so focused on the war that they failed to see the truth: the Sith were the masterminds behind the conflict. A dark smokescreen had clouded their vision.

ORDER 66

The chilling truth was that the Sith Master was hidden in the very heart of the Republic. Supreme Chancellor Palpatine was actually Darth Sidious.

At last the moment arrived that Palpatine had been planning for so long. He transmitted Order 66 to his fiercely loyal clone troopers - a command that identified the Jedi as traitors to the Republic.

Across the galaxy, clone troopers opened fire against their Jedi generals. It was a nothing less than a massacre.

Many great Jedi were killed in the first battle of the Clone Wars on Geonosis. Reinforcements, in the form of the Republic's new military, secured a victory against the Separatists.

THE NEW JEDI ORDER

After many years of the Empire's tyrannical rule, Luke Skywalker was taken into the Jedi fold. He was well past the traditional age requirements, for he was already an adult when he first picked up his lightsaber. However, his raw talent in the Force was such that his age did not matter. Young Skywalker was now the galaxy's greatest hope.

THE SITH ORDER

Darth Vader became the terror of the galaxy, carrying out the orders of his Master with unswerving devotion, loyal only to the cruel tenets of the Sith order.

Darth Sidious was apprentice to Darth Plagueis, a wise Sith Lord who, it was rumoured, could control the essence of life. By Sith tradition, Sidious killed Plagueis in his ascent to Master from apprentice.

THE DARK LORDS OF THE SITH

-5100	Marka Ragnos
-5000	Naga Sadow
-4400	Freedon Nadd
-3997	Exar Kun and Ulic Qel-Droma
-3958	Darth Revan and Darth Malak
-3956	Darth Bandon
-3951	Darth Sion, Darth Nihilus, Darth Traya
-1000	Darth Bane and his apprentice Darth Zannah
< -82	Darth Plagueis
-82	Darth Sidious
-54	Darth Maul
-32	Darth Tyranus
-19	Darth Vader

IDENTITY FILE

The Sith was an ancient order devoted to the dark side of the Force and determined to destroy the Jedi. They wished to use the Force for personal gain and oppressive control. Always only two in number, these masters of evil were consumed with their destructive goals. The menace of the Sith was discounted by the Jedi, who thought that it was extinct.

ANCIENT HISTORY

Long before the Republic rose, there lived a culture on the planet Korriban. These primitive people were called the Sith, and the Force flowed strongly through their bloodlines. Although they didn't practice the Force as the Jedi would, they were talented in their own brand of magic.

In the early days of the Jedi, a great divide tore the order apart. A number of Jedi tapped into the forbidden power of the Force's dark side. They rebelled and were exiled from the Republic. Beyond the borders of the Republic, these castaways discovered Korriban and the Sith people.

Powerful with the dark side, the Jedi outcasts set themselves up as gods on Korriban. The primitive Sith worshipped them, and the Dark Jedi built temples and monuments to celebrate their power. After millennia of interbreeding, and the term 'Sith' came to describe not only the indigenous people of Korriban, but also the powerful overlords that ruled them.

During the Sith Empire's golden age, a Republic explorer vessel stumbled upon the secluded world of the Sith. A Sith Lord, Naga Sadow, saw this as a chance to invade the Republic and take revenge on the Jedi who had banished them. This became known as the Great Hyperspace War, and it was the first of many terrible conflicts between Jedi and Sith.

Time and again the Sith and Jedi clashed, with devastated worlds lying in their wake. The last great battle took place on the scarred plains of Ruusan. The Jedi were victorious, but one Sith escaped: Darth Bane.

Darth Bane restructured the cult with duplicity and secrecy in mind, so there could only be two - a Master and an apprentice. Bane adopted cunning, subterfuge and stealth as the basics of the Sith order.

"ANGER... FEAR... AGGRESSION. THE DARK SIDE OF THE FORCE ARE THEY."

HIDING IN THE SHADOWS

The dark side can be extremely hard to detect, even by those who are strong in the Force. Darth Sidious was able to keep his true self a secret, even though he worked in the public glare.

Sidious had been Apprentice to Darth Plagueis, a wise Sith Lord whose knowledge of arcane and unnatural arts was reputed to extend to manipulating the very essence of life. By Sith tradition, Sidious killed Plagueis in his ascent to Master from apprentice.

The fearsome Darth Maul became Sidious' apprentice and launched a blistering attack on the Jedi Master, Qui-Gon Jinn. At first, Qui-Gon's report of a Sith attack was met with hesitation and skepticism. But with the death of Darth Maul at Naboo, the Jedi Council realised that the Sith menace was true. What they didn't know was whether Maul was the Master or the Apprentice.

Count Dooku, a former Jedi, became Sidious' next Apprentice. As Darth Tyranus, Dooku became a political firebrand, fanning the flames of rebellion across the Republic. He engineered the vast armies that would fight on both sides of the Clone Wars: the droid armies of the united Confederacy of Independent Systems and the clone army of the Republic. The Clone Wars were an elaborate and costly sham, which spread the Jedi ranks thin across the galaxy and drew more political power to Darth Sidious.

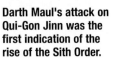

Darth Maul's attack on Qui-Gon Jinn was the first indication of the rise of the Sith Order.

THE REVENGE OF THE SITH

When the time was right, the Jedi were wiped out by their clone soldiers. What few survivors remained were branded as enemies of the state. With Sidious as the Galactic Emperor, and Darth Vader as his new and fanatically loyal apprentice, the Sith ruled the galaxy and plunged it into darkness.

TIME FILES

-5000 THE GREAT HYPERSPACE WAR
At this point in time, the Sith were based on the Outer Rim planet of Korriban, an area that hadn't previously been explored by the Republic. With the defeat of the Sith in this conflict, the period also became known as the fall of the Sith Empire.

~ -4000 THE GREAT SITH WAR
Two fallen Jedi, Exar Kun and Ulic Qel-Droma, became the Dark Lords of the Sith. The Sith and their Mandalorian allies were defeated. Following the devastation of Ossus, the Jedi Temple on Coruscant became one of the major Jedi strongholds.

-3995 THE MANDALORIAN WARS
In the aftermath of the Great Sith War, the Mandalorians went into battle against the Republic. The conflict lasted 34 years. The Jedi and the Republic were victorious, but many in the Republic became disillusioned.

-3958 THE SECOND SITH WAR
Two Jedi war heroes revealed themselves as Dark Lords of the Sith, Darth Revan and Darth Malak. The rift they caused divided the Republic. Two years into the civil war, Darth Revan fell into a Jedi trap. He was captured and his memory was erased. Malak consolidated the forces of the Sith and took on Darth Bandon as his apprentice. Malak's forces decimated the Jedi academy on Dantooine.

-3951 SITH CIVIL WAR
Darth Sion and Darth Kreia began to hunt down the Jedi in secret. The surviving Jedi publicly disbanded, but the Jedi Masters secretly watched over the scattered Jedi. The Sith began a war among themselves.

-1000 THE BATTLE OF RUUSAN
Lord Kaan and his Sith Lords were defeated by Lord Hoth at Ruusan. A new Galactic Republic was formed under the leadership of a democratically elected Supreme Chancellor and a representative government known as the Galactic Senate. The only Sith survivors, Darth Bane and his apprentice Darth Zannah, began plotting in secret to retake the galaxy.

YODA

IDENTITY FILE

Yoda was a venerable Jedi Master who was revered for his wisdom and insight. As one of the most experienced members of the Jedi Council, Yoda's advice held great weight among his peers. Throughout his life, he visited hundreds of worlds in his quest to deepen his understanding of, and connection to, the Force.

Yoda grew thoughtful and deliberate, preferring careful contemplation to rash action. Relying on his strong connection to the Force, he sensed dangerous emotions in Anakin Skywalker that could lead the boy to the dark side.

DANGER!

Twelve years before the Battle of Naboo, Yoda was the target of an assassination attempt. Xanatos and Bruck Chun planted a bomb in the Room of a Thousand Fountains, but Yoda was able to escape unharmed.

A WISE TEACHER

Yoda served a vital role in the Jedi Council. When young Padawans began their first foray into Jedi training, they did so under Yoda's guidance. Many of the Republic's greatest and most revered Jedi trained under Yoda when they were children.

When the Jedi hopefuls entered their teenage years, they would then be paired with an elder Jedi Knight or Master to continue training one-on-one.

Yoda's path to Jedi wisdom seemed simple, and yet it was profound. He made his students unlearn what they had been taught, helping them to tune in to the subtle world around them to learn its truths. He taught them that a Jedi uses the Force for knowledge, never for attack.

GREEN BLOOD

GREEN LIGHTSABER

FIVE TOES;
three at the front and
two towards the back.

THE DEATH OF THE REPUBLIC

When Emperor Palpatine ordered his purge of the Jedi, Yoda went into hiding on Dagobah. He used the Force and the planet's own natural defences to discourage visitors. But he kept a watch on Luke Skywalker and Leia Organa, using the Force to monitor their growth.

Yoda was a Form IV lightsaber combat master, which emphasised acrobatics.

THE LAST OF THE JEDI

By the time Luke Skywalker first encountered Yoda in the bogs of Dagobah, the Jedi Master was nearly 900 years old. He walked with the aid of a stick and lived on those things that nature offered him; he ate plants, fruit and fungi, and built his home of mud, sticks and stones.

At first Luke did not take Yoda seriously. But when the old Jedi Master accepted the challenge of teaching the son of Anakin Skywalker, he was a demanding and inspiring tutor. As Luke performed gruelling physical and mental exercises, Yoda taught him about the Force. He cautioned against the easy path of anger and the lure of the dark side of the Force.

Despite Yoda's warnings, Luke left Dagobah before his training was complete when he sensed that his friends were in danger. By the time Luke returned, Yoda was close to becoming one with the Force. Yoda revealed that a confrontation with Darth Vader and Emperor Palpatine would be necessary for Luke to complete his Jedi training.

Finally, Yoda breathed his last and vanished, becoming one with the Force. Yoda's long life had ended in the flame of his greatest triumph. He had ensured the rebirth of the great Jedi Order.

THE FORCE

Yoda's connection with the Force gave him astounding strength and speed, as well as the ability to levitate. These special powers, combined with his expansive knowledge of fighting tactics, allowed him to defeat virtually any opponent. As the shadow of the dark side fell over the Republic, Yoda grew increasingly concerned. The disturbance in the Force was strong enough to cloud the Jedi's insights into important matters. He could sense that dark and dangerous times lay ahead.

MACE WINDU

During the Battle of Geonosis, Mace Windu beheaded Jango Fett. He later led a group of five commando clone troopers in the battle outside the arena.

IDENTITY FILE

Mace Windu was a highly revered Jedi Master and a senior member of the Jedi Council. By nature he was a diplomat, and he always sought peaceful solutions to the most volatile issues. He spoke with authority and conviction. Like Yoda, he was respected for his profound wisdom and remarkable accomplishments.

DID YOU KNOW?

He invented the Vaapad-style fighting technique.

As a Padawan, he served a tour on Wroona fighting pirates aboard the primitive sailing ship Temblor.

Mace Windu once worked with Republic policing squads to contain the Arkanian Revolution.

He battled Gorm the Dissolver.

A LEGENDARY WARRIOR

Of all the Jedi on the Council, Windu was perhaps the most fearsome warrior. He had complete mastery over Jedi fighting styles. It was said that only two others had ever defeated him in battle - Yoda and Count Dooku. He was calm and collected when faced with death, and willing to sacrifice himself for any just cause. Nothing could dull Windu's fighting edge or his willingness to venture forth on dangerous missions.

Mace was one of the best lightsaber fighters in the Jedi order. Only the most skilled of the Jedi could master his Form VII discipline of combat - the deadly technique known as Vaapad. Its aggressive nature came perilously close to dark side practices.

THE PURPLE LIGHTSABER

One of the many legendary tales revolving around Mace Windu is that of his first solo mission, where he retrieved unique Lightsaber crystals from Hurikane when he was 14 years old. These crystals formed his distinctive purple Lightsaber.

MISSION TO MALASTARE

Shortly after the Battle of Naboo, several Jedi Council members were sent to Malastare to forge a truce between the terrorist group known as the Red Iaro and the people of Lannik. Mace Windu served as the Senior Council member and Acting Director during this mission.

After being attacked by akk dogs on Malastare, he travelled to Nar Shaddaa to learn who had trained them to be killers. To his horror, he discovered that the akk dogs were being illegally used for sport in a Circus Horrificus event hosted by Gargonn the Hutt.

THE JOKER

To some, Mace Windu seemed to be sombre and steady. Yet of all the Jedi, he was quickest to appreciate a joke, and often sprang devious philosophical traps during debates. His creative, whimsical side defied intellectual analysis.

THE CHOSEN ONE

Windu was well schooled in Jedi philosophy and history. He knew of the ancient prophecy of the Chosen One who would return balance to the Force. However, when Qui-Gon Jinn approached the Council with a prospective candidate to fulfill that prophecy, Windu was hesitant. Although Anakin Skywalker had the highest midi-chlorian count on record and showed great potential, the Council and Windu decided that he was not to be trained.

After Qui-Gon's death, the Council rescinded their original decision, but Windu continued to feel a mistrust of Skywalker, sensing that he was too powerful for his age and too unpredictable.

THE CLONE WARS

Windu was a diplomat by nature and he believed strongly in the power of words over action. But as the galaxy found itself increasingly fragmented by the rise of the powerful secessionist movement, he grew to question some of his firmest held beliefs.

As the Clone Wars erupted on Geonosis, Windu led a special squad of commando clone troopers into the thick of battle. He was one of the few Jedi to return unscathed from that first engagement.

In the later years of the Republic, Windu spent most of his time in the Jedi Temple, conferring with Yoda and the ten other members of the Council, and contemplating the very nature of the Force.

Mace Windu became a member of the High Council at the age of 28. His adventurous exploits were an inspiration to his fellow Jedi, and he led through rigorous example and steady discipline.

A NOBLE DEATH

Windu felt uncertain about the direction of the Republic. He grew to distrust Supreme Chancellor Palpatine, and his concern was justified. Chancellor Palpatine was Darth Sidious, the Sith Lord that had escaped Jedi detection all this time. It was Anakin Skywalker who loyally delivered news of this discovery to Windu, though the Jedi Master still did not fully trust the young Jedi.

When Mace went to arrest the Chancellor, Palpatine dropped the disguise of harmless politician and revealed himself as the deadly Sith Lord he really was. Although Windu disarmed and cornered Sidious, his mistrust of Anakin was proven justified. Skywalker sheared off Mace Windu's weapon hand before he could strike Palpatine.

Sidious bombarded the defenceless Windu with Sith lightning. The final blast hurled him into the Coruscant skies, and he fell to his death.

Palpatine attacked Mace Windu with forked bolts of Sith lightning. They penetrated Mace's body, illuminating him from within.

KI-ADI-MUNDI

Ki-Adi-Mundi was an alien representative who sat on the Jedi Council. A humanoid being, Ki's most distinguishing physical feature was an enlarged conical cranium that contained a binary brain.

IDENTITY FILE

Master Ki-Adi-Mundi was a thoughtful Cerean, with a binary brain supported by a second heart. He accompanied Mace Windu on their desperate mission to Geonosis to subdue the Separatists and their ever-expanding droid armies. Ki-Adi-Mundi became a Republic General in the Clone Wars because of his keen insight and natural leadership abilities.

DID YOU KNOW?

Ki-Adi-Mundi was trained in the Jedi arts by Master Yoda himself.

Because of the low birthrate of Cereans, Ki-Adi-Mundi was exempt from the Jedi edict that discouraged marriage.

During the Clone Wars, Ki-Adi-Mundi lost his entire family.

Ki-Adi-Mundi voyaged to Naboo to attend Qui-Gon Jinn's funeral. He was also present at the jubilant celebration that marked the liberation of Naboo.

MYSTERIOUS BEGINNINGS

Ki-Adi-Mundi embarked on the Jedi's path when he was four years old. Although few children were allowed into the Jedi Temple beyond the age of about six months, a mysterious Jedi Master known as the "Dark Woman" had heard of Ki-Adi-Mundi's powerful ability to manipulate objects with his mind. She arrived at Ki's home on Cerea and asked for permission to take the child with her to Coruscant.

Ki's family was tormented by a band of raiders under the leadership of Bin-Garda-Zon. Ki's father hid his son for fear that the bandit lord would kidnap the boy, as male children were scarce on Cerea. When Bin-Garda-Zon and the raiders eventually left, Ki's father agreed to send Ki with the Dark Woman.

OLD ENEMIES

After 21 years, Ki-Adi-Mundi, now a Jedi Knight, returned to Cerea to rid the planet of the bandits. He sought out Bin-Garda-Zon's camp, only to discover that the legendary bandit leader had been deposed by a female warrior. Ki defeated her, but his adventure was not yet over. Bin-Garda-Zon made a pitiful attempt to kill Ki. The Jedi vanquished him, but spared his life.

When Chancellor Palpatine initiated Order 66, the ultimate endgame contingency against the Jedi, Ki-Adi-Mundi was on the Banking Clan stronghold world of Mygeeto. Commander Bacara and his marines opened fire on the Jedi Master. Although he attempted to put up a defence, he was overwhelmed by the gunfire and killed.

RESCUE

Shortly before the Battle of Naboo, Ki-Adi-Mundi became embroiled in a political struggle on Cerea.

The Pro-Tech Movement, led by a human named Bron, advocated the introduction of new technology to Cerea, which Ki-Adi-Mundi and other older Cereans opposed. One of Ki's daughters, Sylvn, became involved in the movement. When a criminal named Ephant Mon kidnapped Sylvn, Ki-Adi-Mundi tracked them to Jabba the Hutt's lair on the desert world of Tatooine. He rescued his daughter and learned that the Trade Federation was purchasing weapons to arm their starships.

DRAGON SLAYER

A short time after the Trade Federation's defeat, the Jedi Council sent Ki-Adi-Mundi to Tatooine in search of a Jedi Master named Sharad Hett, who had vanished years before and was living among the Tusken Raiders. When he reached the desert world, Ki again crossed paths with Jabba the Hutt. Jabba promised not to interfere with Ki's mission and even provided him with eight bodyguards and a desert skiff.

However, when the skiff encountered a sandstorm, Jabba's henchmen piloted the skiff into the heart of the storm, then turned on Ki and tried to kill him. The skiff crashed, tossing Jabba's thugs and the Jedi, into the desert. The skiff, all of Jabba's henchmen and the Jedi were buried in the sandstorm.

Ki suffered a broken arm, but used the Force to accelerate the healing process after escaping the sand. Wounded and low on supplies, Ki attempted to cross the Jundland Wastes. He braved the terrible heat and womp rat attacks until finally stumbling into a krayt dragon's lair.

Hett and his band had also arrived at the cave and leapt to the Jedi's rescue. Ki-Adi-Mundi seriously wounded the creature by applying a torch to its soft, unprotected underbelly. Finally, Ki, Hett and his son A'Sharad struck together and killed the krayt dragon.

Although Ki-Adi-Mundi had found the missing Jedi, his mission was complicated by the arrival of the bounty hunter Aurra Sing. A failed Jedi apprentice who once trained under the Dark Woman, Sing now revelled in killing all Jedi. Ki-Adi-Mundi could not prevent the bounty hunter from slaying the reclusive Jedi Master. As Hett died, Ki vowed to take his son, A'Sharad, as his Padawan.

THE CLONE WARS

A year after the outbreak of the Clone Wars, Ki-Adi-Mundi found himself in a dangerous situation on Aargonar. A'Sharad Hett had been shot down in battle and Obi-Wan Kenobi was presumed killed. With the help of Anakin Skywalker, Ki-Adi-Mundi's forces were able to turn the tide. With Obi-Wan gone, the Jedi Council temporarily reassigned Anakin to Ki-Ai-Mundi. They were sent to deal with the increasing pirate activity in the Varonat system. There, Anakin sensed through the Force that Obi-Wan was still alive. Disobeying Ki-Adi-Mundi's orders, he left for Riflor, where he found Obi-Wan alive. Having had enough of the headstrong, reckless Padawan, Ki-Adi-Mundi happily returned responsibility for training and guiding Anakin to Master Kenobi.

THE SENATE

The Senate consisted of elected leaders from the worlds throughout the Republic. Some senators represented only a single world, but there were also a number of sectorial senators who represented multiple worlds within the same sector.

IDENTITY FILE

Finis Valorum was a well-meaning politician, but he was no match for the machinations of those working behind the scenes to bring him down. He came from a long line of influential politicians, and his family dynasty could be traced back thousands of years.

Valorum had skill as a politician, but he had no charisma. He did not know how to deflect attacks upon his character by the media, and there were many rumours about how his family stood to profit from taxation.

On the advice of his colleague, Senator Palpatine of Naboo, Valorum backed the taxation of Free Trade Zones in the Republic. When the Trade Federation blockaded Naboo in protest, many people blamed Valorum.

Supreme Chancellor Finis Valorum was one of the last to hold that office before the collapse of the Galactic Republic and the rise of the cruel Empire.

The Senate building was a massive dome. A mighty courtyard that led to the building was lined with sculptures of the Republic's founders. Inside its lavender-coloured walls, each Senatorial delegation had huge banks of office space customised to its cultural environment. In total, 1,024 repulsorlift platforms lined Senate rotunda.

THE SENATE

The Galactic Senate existed for thousands of generations, and was one of the founding points of the Galactic Constitution that established the Republic. The Senate was comprised of a body of senators who represented the many worlds of the galaxy. Together they governed the Galactic Republic.

Inside the awesome Senate building, hundreds of politicians were crammed into the viewing platforms that lined the curved walls. When a senator wished to speak, the platform would detach and float to the centre of the auditorium. In this way, the senators could easily address all their colleagues at the same time.

At first the Senate was made up of wise and dedicated senators. But as the Republic grew, so did deceit and corruption. The Republic began to rot from within. Many of the senators greedily sought wealth and influence by exploiting a system that was too bureaucratic and slow to stop them.

THE BEGINNING OF THE END

After the Trade Federation blockaded Naboo, Supreme Chancellor Valorum was eager to help resolve the situation peacefully. Ignoring usual procedure, he sent two Jedi ambassadors on a secret mission to negotiate an end to the crisis. However, the negotiations failed because the Trade Federation attacked the ambassadors before talks could even begin.

With the help of the Jedi, Queen Amidala of the Naboo travelled to Coruscant to present her case to the Senate and to ask for their support. She wanted them to order the Trade Federation to leave her home. But Valorum was helpless to assist her, because in the Senate hall he had to abide by the official bureaucratic measures.

The Trade Federation denied Queen Amidala's claims of invasion and demanded that a commission should investigate the accusation. Alarmed and frustrated, the Queen took the advice of her ambassador Palpatine. She launched a stinging verbal attack on Valorum for his inability to take action, and called for a Vote of No Confidence in his rule.

The vote was soon seconded, and Valorum was voted out of power. Palpatine was voted in to succeed him. The Senate had no way of knowing that they were playing into the hands of the wicked Sith Lord Darth Sidious. Everything was going according to his plan.

LOSS OF POWER

When Palpatine declared himself Emperor and the Clone Wars ended, he created a new system of regional governors. This gave him tighter control over all the territories of the galaxy, under the pretence of increased security measures. By the time of the Galactic Civil War, the Senate was no more.

PALPATINE

IDENTITY FILE

Palpatine rose to power through cunning, deception and treachery. As a Sith apprentice he was instructed in the dark side of the Force by Darth Plagueis the Wise. After murdering his master, Palpatine began plotting his rise to power.

As Supreme Chancellor, Palpatine promised to put an end to corruption in the Senate. However, the Republic descended further into chaos. A decade after his inauguration, the Separatist movement threatened the fragile unity of the Republic. The Senate gave Chancellor Palpatine emergency powers and he ordered the Republic's new clone army into operation.

Palpatine was a master public speaker and stood for a simple set of ideals. Appealing to the majority at times of uncertainty, he made sure that he had support within the Senate until the time came for him to seize absolute power.

Palpatine was representative for his home planet of Naboo in the Galactic Senate. When Queen Amidala moved for a Vote of No Confidence in the leadership, Palpatine was elected Supreme Chancellor.

CRISIS ON NABOO

Senator Palpatine came from the planet of Naboo, an idyllic world close to the Outer Rim Territories. When taxes were increased on outlying trade routes, the powerful Trade Federation carried out a blockade of the planet. They cut off all supplies and made hostages of the elected rulers, Queen Amidala and Governor Sio Bibble.

After her rescue by Qui-Gon Jin and Obi-Wan Kenobi, Queen Amidala travelled to the seat of the government on the planet of Coruscant to call for intervention by the Galactic Senate. Senator Palpatine convinced her to move for a Vote of No Confidence in the Republic's leadership. There was much sympathy within the Senate for the people of Naboo and Palpatine was elected the new Supreme Chancellor. He promised strong leadership and an end to corruption.

Palpatine had been very devious and was in league with the Trade Federation all along. They knew him only as Darth Sidious, a mysterious Sith Lord who appeared to them via hologram. Darth Sidious instructed the Trade Federation to carry out the blockade and to invade Naboo. This created an atmosphere of political tension that could only result in the downfall of the government.

Emperor Palpatine created a New Order, the Galactic Empire. He ruled the galaxy through tyranny and fear, using a vast military to crush any rebellion.

THE CHOSEN ONE

A young slave boy, Anakin Skywalker, was believed to be the prophesized Chosen One who would bring balance to the Force. Palpatine's intuition led him to keep a close eye on the boy and, over the years, a friendship formed between the two.

During his development as a Jedi and as a man, Anakin came to rely on Chancellor Palpatine's counsel. This relationship exposed Anakin to the seductive nature of the Dark Side of the Force. Where the Jedi would impose self-restraint, Palpatine encouraged Anakin to give way to passion. Where the Jedi practised humility, Palpatine flattered Anakin's ego. Palpatine became a close confidant and knew all about the secrets that Anakin hid from his Jedi peers, including his marriage to Padmé Amidala.

Padmé fell pregnant and Anakin began to foresee her death in his dreams. Palpatine seized this chance and revealed his true nature as a Sith Lord to Anakin. He offered to teach Anakin the means to save Padmé's life through knowledge of the Dark Side of the Force. Anakin's acceptance would have a devastating effect on the Jedi Order and the Galactic Republic.

His true nature as the Sith Lord, Darth Sidious, was hidden from the Galactic Senate and the Jedi Order.
Under the influence of Darth Sidious the Trade Federation invaded Naboo.

THE NEW ORDER

After the death of Darth Maul, Palpatine needed a new apprentice. He chose the Jedi Master Count Dooku and lured him to the Dark Side. As Darth Tyranus, Dooku was charged with creating a clone army to serve the Republic. In Palpatine's future scheme he would have Dooku lead a Separatist movement of such scale that the clone army would be called to arms.

The emergency powers granted to Chancellor Palpatine to activate the clone army were enough to see him stay in power throughout the Clone Wars between the Republic and the Separatists. As the Clone Wars drew to a close he was ready to make one final play to guarantee his position of absolute power in the galaxy.

The clone army served to uphold the Republic at all costs. At last, Palpatine was ready to use Order 66, which would eliminate the Jedi. Clone commanders across the galaxy received the instruction that the Jedi were seeking to undermine the Republic and were to be terminated immediately. With the Jedi all but wiped out, Palpatine abolished the Republic in favour of the First Galactic Empire. He appointed himself Emperor

THE DEATH STAR

Emperor Palpatine ruled ruthlessly and without mercy. Rebellions were swept away by the might of Palpatine's war machine, a vast Imperial fleet of Star Destroyers and TIE starfighters. The Emperor's new apprentice, Darth Vader, and the Imperial commanders spread fear and tyranny throughout the galaxy.

In opposition to the Empire, a Rebel Alliance formed and its numbers grew as the injustices of the Empire increased. Palpatine, as always, had devised a plan many years before to crush a rebellion of any size. In the last days of the Republic he had secretly commissioned a super battle station to be built. The Death Star was the size of a small moon and had the fire power to destroy entire planets.

The Rebel Alliance stole the plans to the Death Star. Anakin Skywalker's son, Luke, managed to destroy it and some important members of the Imperial fleet. Palpatine's evil knew no bounds as he had a second, larger Death Star built, capable of more terror. In the meantime he would have the Rebels, and in particular the young Skywalker, pursued across the galaxy.

However, Luke Skywalker's strength in the Force signalled the end of Palpatine's reign of terror. Young Skywalker turned his father away from the Dark Side, and Darth Vader flung Palpatine into the Death Star's reactor core.

DARTH MAUL

Darth Maul was a Sith lord who embraced the powers of the dark side and served the evil Darth Sidious. Darth Maul's face was a terrifying mask of bizarre ritual combat tattoos. Sharp horns formed a crown around his bald head, and his ferocious yellow eyes revealed a spirit twisted by rage. His eyes were more sensitive to light than a human's, but could strike terror into the hearts of his enemies.

Maul was trained in secret by Sidious, and wielded a double-bladed Lightsaber with animal grace. He was driven by a passionate hatred of the Jedi Order. After savagely murdering Qui-Gon Jinn, he clashed with Obi-Wan Kenobi, who eventually destroyed him.

Maul's Sith Infiltrator was a modified star courier vessel, which was equipped with a cloaking device.

TIME FILE

-33.5	Mission to Dorvalla
-32.5	Infiltrates Black Sun
-32.5	Given the Sith Infiltrator
-32	Kills Mahwi Lihnn and Hath Monchar
-32	Kills Anoon Bondara, Darsha Assant
-32	Kills Lorn Pavan
-32	Tracks Queen Amidala to Tatooine
-32	First encounter with Qui-Gon Jinn
-32	Battle of Naboo
-32	Kills Qui-Gon Jinn
-32	Killed by Obi-Wan Kenobi

TRAINING

Darth Maul's dark past was shrouded in mystery. He trained under Darth Sidious, learning the esoteric art of fighting with a double-bladed lightsaber. It is believed that he undertook various covert missions for his master, leaving the Jedi completely unaware of his existence prior to his first meeting with Qui-Gon Jinn on Tatooine. Sidious sent Maul to kill Qui-Gon and Obi-Wan Kenobi and recapture Queen Amidala.

SHIP AND WEAPONS

Maul's mode of transport was his Sith Infiltrator, a deadly starship with a cloaking device. During scouting missions and pursuits, he mounted a Sith speeder. He intended to strike terror into the hearts of his enemies, and he used a variety of blood-chilling weapons in the service of his wicked master. His weapon of choice was the double-bladed lightsaber, which he would wield effectively with either or both blades ignited. A small group of Sith probe droids assisted him in his cruel plots.

HOME PLANET

Darth Maul was originally a Zabrak from Iridonia, but he abandoned every trace of his former life when he took on his Sith name.

DEFEAT AND DEATH

The powerful Jedi Knight Obi-Wan Kenobi relied upon the power of the Force to vanquish Darth Maul. After losing his own lightsaber, Obi-Wan found himself dangling just above a deep melting pit. Using the Force, he leapt from the pit and called Qui-Gon's weapon to his hand. Maul paused in surprise, and his pause cost him his life. He was cut in two and flung deep into the melting pit.

"AT LAST WE WILL REVEAL OURSELVES TO THE JEDI. AT LAST WE WILL HAVE REVENGE."

Maul's speeder was pared down and unarmed. Maul had customised it and stripped it down to the bare essentials to achieve maximum speed capacity.

The dark warrior Darth Maul was devoted to the Sith cause with his entire being. He endured the agony of having ritualistic combat tattoos applied all over his body, and his devotion to his master, Darth Sidious, was absolute. He operated as a killing machine of pure evil, carrying out his missions from the shadows.

EARLY YEARS

Darth Maul was turned into a deadly weapon through harsh, abusive training and physical and mental challenges. As part of Maul's training, Darth Sidious sent him to a planet in the Outer Rim. For nearly a month, Maul was hounded by assassin droids, battling with every ounce of his strength and determination in desert conditions, swamps and mountain terrains. His final challenge was to battle Sidious himself.

After the training, Sidious and Maul visited the Sith archives, where they located the designs for what would become Darth Maul's double-bladed lightsaber.

FIGHTING STYLE

Early in his life, Darth Maul learned the intricate movements and forms of the teräs käsi fighting style. One of his earliest memories was that of being taken to the Jedi Temple by Darth Sidious to watch their enemies as they entered and exited the building. He spent many long days carefully forging the crystals used to build his lightsaber. Sidious considered Maul's pride to be his greatest weakness.

QUI-GON JINN

The kind and enlightened Qui-Gon Jinn was a dedicated Jedi Master. He trained Obi-Wan Kenobi and discovered young Anakin Skywalker on Tatooine. His peers saw him as something of a rebel, but he was strongly connected to the Living Force. Qui-Gon had great compassion and empathy for other living things, and he was considered by all to be noble and wise. He was still an accomplished warrior and wielded his lightsaber with grace and skill.

Qui-Gon was a maverick but accomplished Jedi Master who believed in living for the moment. He encouraged others to feel rather than think, and to use their instincts. Although he had some unruly views, he was greatly respected by the other Jedi as a wise student of the Living Force.

TIME FILE

-92	Year of birth	-33	Attends Eriadu trade summit
-82	Becomes Count Dooku's Padawan	-32	Mission to Naboo
-67	Becomes a Jedi Knight	-32	Discovers Anakin Skywalker
-44	Obi-Wan becomes his Padawan	-32	Killed by Darth Maul
-37	Mission to Ord Mantell		

A NEW PADAWAN

Years later, Xanatos tried to trap Qui-Gon on Tatooine. Qui-Gon disrupted Xanatos's plot with the aid of Obi-Wan Kenobi, a Jedi hopeful whom Qui-Gon had previously refused to take as his Padawan learner. Xanatos escaped, but Qui-Gon had overcome his sense of failure. He agreed to train Obi-Wan, and together they made a formidable team.

FAILURE AND CRISIS

Qui-Gon Jinn's early career as a Jedi was marked by a tremendous failure. He took a Jedi hopeful named Xanatos as his Padawan. Xanatos was from Telos and was born with a high midi-chlorian count, but he was a difficult student who used his high birth in attempts to impress other students at the Jedi Temple.

Despite his obvious flaws, Xanatos proved a dedicated student who always sought to learn more about the ways of the Force and please his Master. But when Qui-Gon and his Padawan returned to Telos, Xanatos joined forces with his father in an attempt to take control of the planet. Qui-Gon soon found himself battling his student in a dangerous civil war.

Qui-Gon was eventually forced to kill Xanatos's father in battle. Xanatos immediately attacked his Master. Qui-Gon defeated him, but could not bear to kill the boy. Xanatos fled and disappeared. Haunted by this betrayal and his own failure, Qui-Gon refused to take another Padawan learner.

Qui-Gon had great skill with a lightsaber, but his prowess was no match for the lightning-fast Darth Maul. After Maul struck him down during their mighty duel on Naboo, the Sith Lord was killed by Obi-Wan Kenobi. But it was too late to save the noble Qui-Gon Jinn.

A LEGENDARY PARTNERSHIP

Qui-Gon and Obi-Wan had many adventures together throughout the galaxy. Many years before the Battle of Naboo, the Jedi travelled to civil-war-torn Melida/Daan to find a Jedi who had been captured by one of the warring factions. With the aid of a group of tunnel dwellers called the Young, they rescued their Jedi comrade. But when Qui-Gon returned to Coruscant, Obi-Wan went against his master's wishes and remained on the planet to fight alongside the Young. Eventually Qui-Gon returned to Melida/Daan to help settle the dispute and to be reunited with his Padawan. With Qui-Gon's help, the warring groups were able to settle their differences, ending the last battle of Zehava.

Qui-Gon discovered a young slave boy called Anakin Skywalker on the Outer Rim world of Tatooine. He sensed that the boy was strong in the Force, and liberated him from slavery. When the Jedi Council refused to train him, Qui-Gon kept the boy as his ward.

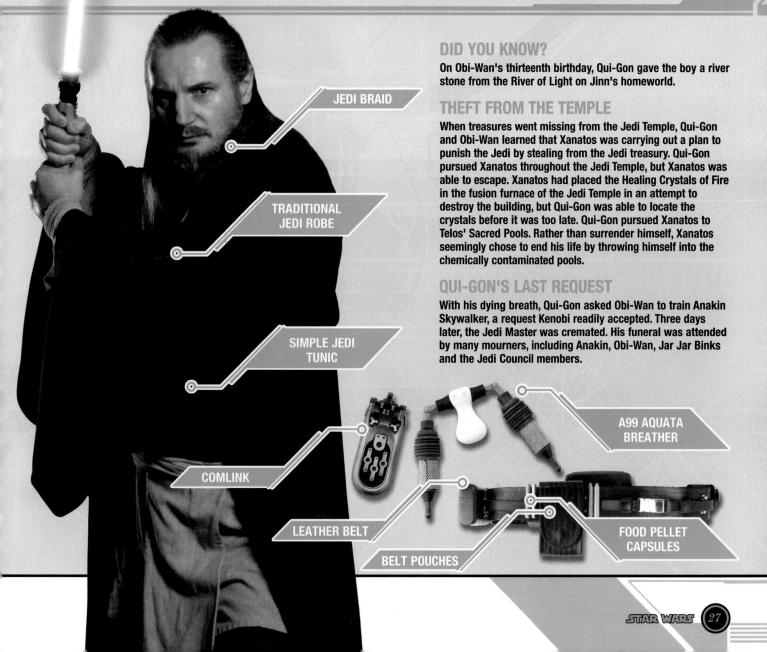

DID YOU KNOW?

On Obi-Wan's thirteenth birthday, Qui-Gon gave the boy a river stone from the River of Light on Jinn's homeworld.

THEFT FROM THE TEMPLE

When treasures went missing from the Jedi Temple, Qui-Gon and Obi-Wan learned that Xanatos was carrying out a plan to punish the Jedi by stealing from the Jedi treasury. Qui-Gon pursued Xanatos throughout the Jedi Temple, but Xanatos was able to escape. Xanatos had placed the Healing Crystals of Fire in the fusion furnace of the Jedi Temple in an attempt to destroy the building, but Qui-Gon was able to locate the crystals before it was too late. Qui-Gon pursued Xanatos to Telos' Sacred Pools. Rather than surrender himself, Xanatos seemingly chose to end his life by throwing himself into the chemically contaminated pools.

QUI-GON'S LAST REQUEST

With his dying breath, Qui-Gon asked Obi-Wan to train Anakin Skywalker, a request Kenobi readily accepted. Three days later, the Jedi Master was cremated. His funeral was attended by many mourners, including Anakin, Obi-Wan, Jar Jar Binks and the Jedi Council members.

JEDI BRAID

TRADITIONAL JEDI ROBE

SIMPLE JEDI TUNIC

COMLINK

A99 AQUATA BREATHER

LEATHER BELT

FOOD PELLET CAPSULES

BELT POUCHES

OBI-WAN KENOBI

TIME FILE

-57	Year of birth
-44	Becomes Jedi Padawan to Qui-Gon Jinn
-32	Qui-Gon and Obi-Wan travel to Naboo to settle a trade dispute
-32	Death of Qui-Gon Jinn
-32	Kills Darth Maul
-32	Becomes a Jedi Knight
-32	Takes Anakin Skywalker as his Padawan
-22	Discovers clone army being created on Kamino
-22	Battle of Geonosis
-19	Mission at Coruscant to rescue Supreme Chancellor Palpatine
-19	Defeats General Grievous on Utapau
-19	Duels with Anakin on Mustafar
-19	Delivers Luke Skywalker to the Lars family on Tatooine
0	Introduces Luke Skywalker to the Force
0	Mission to Alderaan
0	Becomes one with the Force during a duel with Darth Vader
3	As a spirit, tells Luke to go to Dagobah to meet Yoda
4	As a spirit, is reunited with Yoda and Anakin Skywalker

IDENTITY FILE

As a young man, Obi-Wan was headstrong and bold. He was heavily influenced by the teachings of many leading Jedi, including Yoda. In battle he was quick and agile, but he lacked Qui-Gon's deep empathy for other living creatures. After Qui-Gon was killed by Darth Maul, Obi-Wan used his ingenuity and mastery over the Force to defeat the evil Sith lord. He then swore an oath to take Anakin Skywalker as his own Padawan, regardless of the Jedi Council's reservations about the boy's future.

MYSTERY MISSION

Just before the blockade of Naboo, Obi-Wan volunteered to search for fellow Padawan Darsha Assant, with whom he had once shared a mission. He travelled to the Crimson Corridor, hunting for clues. Eventually he made a grim discovery - the melted hilt of Darsha's lightsaber.

Obi-Wan returned to the Jedi Temple with the news and found Qui-Gon Jinn preparing for their mission to Naboo. Obi-Wan knew that the mystery behind Darsha's death would have to wait. He could have had no idea that this would be his last mission alongside Qui-Gon.

HIS MASTER'S WEAPON

After Qui-Gon's death at the hands of Darth Maul, Obi-Wan used the green lightsaber that used to belong to his Master.

AN EXTRAORDINARY PADAWAN

Obi-Wan soon discovered that with Anakin, the boundaries between Master and Apprentice were often erased. He was learning from the boy almost as much as the boy was learning from him. But Obi-Wan's lack of experience as a teacher, combined with his proud refusal to seek help or advice, resulted in his failure to see that Anakin was being lured closer and closer to the dark side of the Force.

Although Obi-Wan fought and overcame Anakin Skywalker on the volcanic planet of Mustafar, the experience was heartbreaking for him. He had always believed that the boy was the prophesied 'Chosen One' who would bring balance to the Force. Now he had to accept that he had failed in his responsibility to guide Anakin, and the entire Galaxy would suffer the consequences.

"I HAVE FAILED YOU, ANAKIN. I WAS NEVER ABLE TO TEACH YOU TO THINK."

THE RISE OF THE SITH

When Obi-Wan finally realised what was happening to Anakin, he was horrified. He tried to turn Skywalker back to the light side, but by then it was too late. After a ferocious lightsaber battle, Obi-Wan cut off Anakin's arms and legs and left him to burn in the molten lava.

During the terror and confusion of the rise of the Sith, Obi-Wan helped to hide the twin children born to Anakin's wife. The baby girl, Leia, was entrusted to Bail Organa while the boy, Luke, was given to Owen Lars and his wife Beru to raise as their nephew. Neither child was to be told of their true parentage.

AN OLD FRIEND

After many long years, Obi-Wan duelled once again with his old Padawan. He felt as though Darth Vader was a different person from the boy that he had trained, and he did not believe that a shred of the old Anakin Skywalker remained within the evil Sith Lord. They engaged in a fierce lightsaber duel.

Eventually, seeing the need for a diversion, Kenobi let himself be struck by Vader's lightsaber. However, his cloak fell empty to the floor, because he had become one with the Force.

LUKE'S MENTOR

Obi-Wan's death did not stop him from being Luke's mentor and protector. He continued to guide Luke, eventually directing him towards the planet Dagobah to continue his training under Jedi Master Yoda. He appeared to Luke many times more as the boy continued to train as a Jedi. Although he had failed to help Anakin, he ultimately succeeded in destroying the Empire through his support of Anakin's son.

Obi-Wan Kenobi was a cautious and disciplined Jedi, who became Anakin Skywalker's mentor and master. His resourcefulness and loyalty led the Jedi Council to place great trust in him, and he was sent on several secret and important missions by them.

During the Clone Wars, Obi-Wan became a general and fought alongside Bail Organa of Alderaan. After the collapse of the Republic, he went into hiding on Tatooine so that he could watch over Luke Skywalker. To the outside world he seemed no more than a crazy recluse, but he remained a Jedi of powerful inner focus.

OBI-WAN IN HIDING

Obi-Wan kept track of Luke Skywalker's progress, but the Lars family did not want him to interfere in the boy's life. Owen Lars foiled an early attempt by Obi-Wan to give Luke his father's first lightsaber. Kenobi stayed hidden in the wasteland as the Empire sought out and killed most of the galaxy's remaining Jedi Knights. He brooded constantly about his failures in the training of Anakin Skywalker. He could only hope that Luke might one day fulfil his destiny and destroy the Empire.

GALACTIC REPUBLIC

The Old Republic was ruled by the Galactic Senate. The Senate was made up of representatives from planets across the galaxy.

IDENTITY FILE

The Old Republic was a democratic union that governed the galaxy for thousands of years. It was legendary in its power and reach, but many of the Senators that ran it were corrupt or weak. While corruption began to rot the Republic government, the vast armies and navies were downscaled, and the Republic came to rely on the Jedi Knights more and more for the maintenance of civility.

DID YOU KNOW?

The Republic was created with the signing of the Galactic Constitution on Coruscant more than 25,000 years ago.

THE GREAT HYPERSPACE WAR

Throughout the rein of the Republic, there were many galactic conflicts, including the Hundred-Year Darkness, the Great Droid Rebellion and the Vultar Cataclysm. Over and over again, it was the job of the Jedi Knights and the ancient armies and navies of the Republic to defend against violence.

The Great Hyperspace War was one of the Republic's most destructive conflicts. A forgotten menace, the long-banished Sith Empire, launched an attack on Republic space. Many worlds were forever scarred in that battle, but the Jedi were able to drive back the invaders.

THE DEFEAT OF THE SITH

A thousand years after the Great Hyperspace War, Sith acolytes sparked the Great Sith War. Again, the Jedi and the Republic banded together to fight against the insatiable Sith lust for conquest.

Three millennia later, at the Battle of Ruusan. the Jedi Army of Light and the Sith Brotherhood of Darkness fought again. The Jedi were victorious and believed that the Sith had been destroyed. Many in the galaxy saw this battle as the last of the great wars, and the start of a new era of peace and stability in the Republic.

CORRUPTION AND CONFUSION

As the Republic grew more and more powerful, a large number of Senators grew corrupt or complacent. The bureaucracy that had grown and festered over millennia blocked any attempt at effective government. Many Senators had personal agendas and cared more about themselves than the people they represented. Although the Jedi tried to protect justice and peace, the once-noble Republic began to crumble.

AN AMBITIOUS SENATOR

Senator Palpatine from Naboo stepped into this political mire. His homeworld was under siege by the greedy Trade Federation. Despite the full-scale invasion of the planet, the call to react was tied up in procedure. Queen Amidala called for a Vote of No Confidence in the Supreme Chancellor Valorum, and Palpatine replaced him.

Despite promises of order and compassion, the first decade of Palpatine's term was marked by huge political upheaval. A separatist movement began to split the Republic, and it was all the Jedi could do to maintain order. Ultimately, the legendary Republic would fall and give way to Palpatine's new Imperial order.

DARK TIMES FOR THE GALAXY

Now calling himself 'Emperor', Palpatine revised the Galactic Constitution, and replaced the Old Republic with his New Order. The Jedi Knights, who had tried for so long to keep the galaxy peaceful, were wiped out. The new rule was violent and frightening. Any worlds that rebelled against the New Order were crushed. Those who lived in the protected Core Worlds never saw the worst of the atrocities. Coruscant and Galactic City were renamed Imperial Center and Imperial City.

REBELLION

Out of these oppressive times came the Alliance to Restore the Republic, which was known as the Rebel Alliance. A Galactic Civil War erupted between the Alliance and the Empire.

The Emperor suspended the Senate, thus obliterating the final remains of the Republic.

Four years after the Senate was suspended, the Alliance defeated the Emperor and his evil Empire. The Alliance declared a New Republic and the end of the dark times at last.

JAR JAR BINKS

Jar Jar Binks was from a species of amphibious beings called Gungans that lived in the vast underwater city of Otoh Gunga. Jar Jar was very kind and helpful, but rather clumsy. Seemingly just one step ahead of trouble at all times, he tended to be in a permanently frantic state and his high-pitched voice was always squealing.

He was not even 20 years old by the time he was exiled from Otoh Gunga. By that early age, his clumsiness had resulted in unfortunate incidents with the city sewer system, the accidental freeing of animals in the Otoh Gunga Zoo, and the flooding of the Gungan leader Boss Nass's mansion and adjoining bubbles while he was working as a waiter. His bumbling caused many a headache to city officials.

Jar Jar's fate took a twist when the he encountered a pair of Jedi Knights as they eluded enemy forces during the Trade Federation invasion of Naboo.

THREE FINGERS AND A THUMB ON EACH HAND

THE DEATH OF CAPTAIN TARPALS

Captain Tarpals, a close friend of Jar Jar's, was the officer in charge of escorting Jar Jar away from Otoh Gunga under the Nocombackie Law. Other Gungans referred to Jar Jar as 'The Death of Captain Tarpals' because Tarpals had stood up for him so many times in the past.

PROTRUDING EYES

AMPHIBIAN HEAD

LONG TONGUE

ENCOUNTER WITH A JEDI

After Qui-Gon Jinn fell on Jar Jar, saving him from being trampled by a Trade Federation MTT, Jar Jar swore a life-debt to the Jedi. He guided Qui-Gon and Obi-Wan to Otoh Gunga, even though it meant he'd have to face the unforgiving Boss Nass.

Braving the Nocombackie Law, Jar Jar presented Qui-Gon to Boss Nass, even though he risked the consequence of being 'pounded' to death. Throughout the adventure of liberating Naboo, Jar Jar tagged along with Qui-Gon. Although his bungling, haphazard mannerisms constantly landed him in hot water, his good nature and loyalty somehow helped him triumph in the end.

Queen Amidala requested that Jar Jar make contact with the Gungans. With his help, the Naboo and the Gungans forged an alliance that liberated the besieged world of Naboo.

RUBBERY BODY

LONG FLAT EARS dangling in broad flaps

Jar Jar was a frog-like creature who was banished from his native home, Otoh Gunga. He was kind and peace-loving, but extremely clumsy.

Jar Jar served as Senior Representative of Naboo in the Galactic Senate, alongside Padmé Amidala.

POSITIONS OF RESPONSIBILITY

After Queen Amidala asked Boss Nass and the Gungans for their help in overthrowing the Neimoidians, Boss Nass was convinced that Jar Jar was a great warrior, responsible for bringing the Gungans and the Naboo together. He made Jar Jar a general in the Gungan army. Jar Jar fainted in response. After the Battle of Naboo, Jar Jar Binks rode a wave of Naboo goodwill to become Associate Planetary Representative in the Galactic Senate. The Naboo value purity of heart over other qualifications to govern, often electing juveniles as their rulers. In the case of Jar Jar, they elevated a simple, well-meaning soul to a position that was beyond his abilities. Jar Jar Binks went on to serve as Senior Representative of Naboo in the Galactic Senate. Although he was kind and compassionate, he was also gullible and too trusting. For many, Jar Jar was nothing but a joke, but in the corrupt last years of the Republic, he was a rare example of a non-corrupt politician interested only in the greater good.

EXCERPT FROM CONTEMPORARY NEWS

Representative Jar Jar Binks (Naboo) accidentally destroyed an elaborate ice statue at a gala fundraiser in Coruscant's posh Jrade-district last night. The notoriously maladroit Binks apparently had tucked the tablecloth upon which rested the statue into his cummerbund and pulled down the intricately-crafted Kime Enanrum-original when he attempted to catch tumbling canapés he had knocked from a passing waiter. This incident echoes a similar one two months ago, when Binks accidentally deactivated the sky dome at the opening of the Endangered Shreebird Aviary. "I knew he was invited to attend," said a crestfallen Enanrum, "I don't know what I was thinking even bringing it here."

THE LOYALIST COMMITTEE

Jar Jar was a member of the Loyalist Committee, which was a panel of Senators working to stop the Separatist movement spreading throughout the galaxy. He and Padmé worked hard, favouring negotiation and peaceful resolution over the growing popularity of the Military Creation Act.

A FATAL MISTAKE

When Senator Amidala was forced to leave the capital city because of an assassination attempt, she asked Jar Jar to take her place in the Senate. With the Separatist alliance threatening war, Representative Binks proposed the motion of granting emergency powers to Supreme Chancellor Palpatine. This action would have consequences that were felt not only by the Galactic Republic, but also by the entire galaxy.

BOSS NASS

Boss Rugor Nass was the stout and stern leader of the Gungans. He was extremely proud and believed strongly in maintaining the traditions of his people. He kept a tight rein on Gungan affairs, and did not believe in mixing with the Naboo, with whom the Gungans shared a planet.

His strong will and commanding manner saw him rise to the position of Otoh Gunga's Boss. He had made a name for himself in his younger years, winning the Big Nasty Free-For-All, the most physically demanding event of the Gungan Festival of Warriors, three years in a row.

A cultural misunderstanding led to a rift between the Gungan and the Naboo colonists. This tension was perpetuated by stubbornness and ignorance on both sides. The air was finally cleared by Queen Amidala during the Trade Federation's occupation of Naboo.

INVASION

When the Trade Federation invaded Naboo, Boss Nass chose to remain uninvolved. He thought that they were safe from this surface-dweller's problem. He was wrong. The Trade Federation armies stormed the swamps and forced the Gungans to abandon Otoh Gunga.

The Gungans retreated to a sacred place within the Naboo swamps. There, Queen Amidala, the ruler of the Naboo, pleaded for Boss Nass's help. Stirred by her words, Nass agreed to join forces with the Naboo to rid the planet of the Trade Federation.

THE GUNGANS AND THE NABOO

Nass had an extremely short temper, but he was not completely narrow-minded. Displays of courage and humility could pierce through his preconceptions. When Queen Amidala prostrated herself before him, he was impressed. The Naboo didn't consider themselves superior to the Gungans, after all.

A CHANGE OF POLICY

After striking an alliance with the Naboo, Nass changed his long-standing policy of seclusion, and opened Otoh Gunga to off-world visitors. To preserve the ecological balance of Lake Paonga and the surrounding wilderness, he introduced an initiative to colonise one of Naboo's moons, Ohma-D'un. This marked the first Gungan space exploration, and was a great step forward in joining the culture to the galactic community at large.

Unlike most of the Gungans in Otoh Gunga, Nass was of the old Ankura lineage, shown by his green skin and hooded eyes.

UNDERWATER EXPANSION

Under the conservative rule of Boss Nass, Otoh Gunga flourished and grew. Although Nass was an isolationist, he had grand visions for Otoh Gunga. Eager to make his mark on the city, he commissioned a huge concourse called City Bigspace that proved to be a popular addition to the underwater city.

THE GUNGAN ARMY

Nass committed the Gungan Grand Army to wage war against invading battle droids. When the Trade Federation was driven from Naboo, Nass joined Amidala in a huge celebratory parade that united the Naboo and the Gungans in a new era of peace and cooperation.

THE GUNGANS

EXPRESSIVE FACE

FLEXIBLE SKELETAL STRUCTURE

TALL AND LANKY HUMANOID

STRONG LEG MUSCLES FOR SWIMMING

IDENTITY FILE

The Gungans were the native inhabitants of the planet Naboo. They were ruled by Boss Nass and his Rep Council, from the High Tower Board Room of Otoh Gunga.

The Gungans were an amphibious species with strong lungs capable of holding breath for extended periods. Therefore Gungans were as comfortable in water as they are on land.

RELATIONSHIP WITH THE NABOO

For many years the Gungans had an uneasy relationship with the Naboo, the human colonists on the planet. Many Naboo looked down upon the Gungans, thinking them primitive. The Gungans in turn tried to avoid any contact with the surface-dwellers. Although they had this fundamental failure to understand one another from first contact, it never resulted in warfare between them.

GUNGAN RACES

There were at least two distinct Gungan races. The Otolla Gungan had a tall and lanky build, long ears (or haillu), inquisitive eyes on short stalks and a pronounced bill. The Ankura Gungan was an older race, with a stockier build, shorter bill and haillu, and hooded eyes.

DID YOU KNOW?

Gungans were hatched from eggs in water cradles, and were born as tadpoles. They quickly grew limbs and were able to walk on land within a standard month of hatching.

The power source for Gungan technology was a mysterious blue-white energy 'goo' that was mined in the depths of Naboo's oceans. The viscious plasmic material also formed the basis of Gungan weaponry.

ORGANIC TECHNOLOGY

The Gungans grew the basic structures of buildings, vehicles and technology and adorned them with artistic flourishes and organic lines. This gave Gungan technology a very fluid look.

They mastered energy field technology for a number of uses. Their underwater cities used hydrostatic fields to make large bubbles of atmosphere, within which the Gungans lived.

TRANSPORT

Gungans used beasts for transportation. Their most common mount was the kaadu, a wingless bird that the Gungans adorned with feathers and rode into combat. Other mounts included the large, stubborn falumpaset and the fambaa - a tall, four-legged swamp lizard.

THE GUNGANS AT WAR

The Gungan Grand Army was a huge collection of foot soldiers. They carried cestas, electropoles and atlatls capable of hurling plasmic energy spheres (or boomers, as Gungans call them).

Gungan ground troops carried portable frames that generated a protective energy field. This field was capable of deflecting blaster fire. In large-scale combat, giant Gungan shield generators were able to create a huge umbrella of protective shield energy. This could stop laser bolts and physical objects.

During the Trade Federation invasion, the Grand Army waged an immense ground battle and many Gungans died in the fighting. However, the Queen's forces and allies were able to capture the Trade Federation viceroy, and Naboo was freed.

PEACE ON NABOO

In the festivities that followed their victory, Boss Nass shared a platform with Queen Amidala. A common understanding and love of their world now linked the two cultures forever.

PADMÉ AMIDALA

RIGHT: With the rise of the Separatist movement, Senator Amidala was one of the few who believed in a peaceful resolution to the crisis.

BELOW: As Queen of Naboo, Padmé's elaborate gowns and make-up were steeped with historic symbols important to the Naboo. Her white painted face had stylized beauty marks on her cheeks to display symmetry, and the paint that divided her lower lip was called the 'scar of remembrance', which marked Naboo's time of suffering before the Great Time of Peace.

TIME FILE

-46	Year of birth
-39	Enrolls in Refugee Relief Movement
-38	Joins Apprentice Legislature
-34	Elected Princess of Theed
-33	Falls in love with Palo
-32.5	Elected Queen of Naboo
-32	Trade Federation invades Naboo
-32	Calls for Vote of No Confidence against Valorum
-32	Battle of Naboo
-24.5	Term as Queen ends; becomes Senator
-23	Begins fight against Military Creation Act
-22	Assassination attempts on her life
-22	Battle of Geonosis
-22	Marries Anakin Skywalker
-21	Goes to Ilum
-19.5	Last sees Anakin before he embarks on the Outer Rim Sieges
-19	Tells Anakin that she is pregnant
-19	Anakin dreams of Padmé's death during childbirth
-19	Palpatine turns the Republic into the Empire
-19	Goes to Mustafar to confront Anakin about the attack on the Jedi Temple
-19	Birth of Luke and Leia
-19	Heartbroken over Anakin's fall to the dark side, she dies

IDENTITY FILE

Padmé Naberrie was born in a small mountain village on Naboo. She was identified early as one of Naboo's best and brightest. She served as supervisor of the city of Theed for two years before being elected Queen of Naboo. As per Naboo tradition, she took on the name of state Amidala. After her term as Queen ended, Padmé became a Senator for Naboo, working hard to achieve peace and stability in the galaxy.

Against her self-discipline and pragmatic ideals, Padmé fell in love with the Jedi Padawan Anakin Skywalker. This union would be a key factor in some of the darkest times the galaxy had ever known.

DID YOU KNOW?

Queen Amidala replaced King Veruna, who abdicated the throne in scandal. Amidala was elected in an electronic global election that lasted less than four minutes.

When Anakin ascended to the rank of Jedi Knight, he gave his severed Padawan braid to Padmé. In return, Padmé gave Anakin R2-D2 as his permanent astromech droid.

When in danger, Queen Amidala disguised herself as one of her handmaidens, and adopted her less formal name of Padmé. When disguised as Padmé, her handmaiden Sabé assumed the role of Queen in her place.

During the Trade Federation siege of Naboo, Queen Amidala was rescued by Jedi ambassadors who took her to Coruscant. On the way there, she met Anakin Skywalker, who joined them to go to the Senate. On Coruscant, Amidala called for a Vote of No Confidence in Supreme Chancellor Valorum. Then she returned to Naboo to request aid from the Gungans. Together they brought freedom back to Naboo.

A PEACEFUL SENATOR

When her terms ended, Padmé Amidala became Senator of Naboo, taking the position once occupied by Palpatine. She led the opposition against the Military Creation Act. On the day of the Military Creation Act vote, Amidala's starship was attacked. This led to her being placed under the protection of the Jedi Knights. Amidala was once again reunited with Obi-Wan Kenobi and his Padawan, Anakin Skywalker, whom she had not seen in a decade.

Padmé married Anakin Skywalker in secret.

HEARTBREAK ON MUSTAFAR

When Obi-Wan Kenobi told Padmé that Anakin had turned to the dark side, she travelled to Mustafar to confront Anakin, but Obi-Wan stowed away on her ship.

Anakin had done wicked deeds, believing that they would turn the corrupt Republic into a wonderful empire for their children. He even believed that he could depose Palpatine and make the galaxy exactly what he and Padmé wanted it to be. Padmé was devastated by Anakin's transformation.

When Anakin saw Obi-Wan emerging from Padmé's starship, he thought that she had brought his former Master to kill him. Anakin caught Padmé in a Force chokehold and then tossed her aside. He did not kill her, but he broke her heart.

As Kenobi and Skywalker duelled, C-3PO and R2-D2 carried Padmé aboard her starship. Despite receiving medical care, her life signs continued to dwindle.

SECRET LOVE

Anakin escorted Padmé to Naboo to hide while the Jedi investigated the attacks against her. Anakin and Padmé rekindled an affectionate friendship that had been interrupted ten years prior, and fell in love.

According to the Jedi Code, Anakin could not marry, and Padmé needed to focus on her career. She tried to ignore her feelings, but when their lives were in danger on Geonosis, Padmé declared her love to Anakin. They were rescued by Jedi reinforcements, and then took part in the opening battle of the historic Clone Wars.

After the Battle of Geonosis, Anakin and Padmé were married in a secret ceremony with C-3PO and R2-D2 as their only witnesses.

LIFE AND DEATH

Padmé never knew what had become of Anakin. She never saw the damage he suffered from Kenobi's blade or the lava of Mustafar. She died believing that there was still good within him.

Before slipping away, Padmé gave birth to twins - Leia and Luke. Obi-Wan, Yoda and Bail Organa vowed to keep the children safe.

VISIONS OF THE FUTURE

During the Clone Wars, Anakin became a hero known throughout the Republic. The war was concentrated in the Outer Rim, and Padmé saw very little of him. By the time the Outer Rim Sieges ended, Padmé had stunning news for Anakin – he was going to be a father. Padmé's intuition told her that their baby was a boy, but Anakin suspected it was a girl. He was plagued with terrifying nightmares of Padmé dying during childbirth. He was so scared of losing her that he would have done anything to keep her with him. His fears tempted him towards the dark side, threatening to destroy the lives of those closest to him.

Padmé's body was returned to Naboo. At a state funeral, thousands of Naboo citizens came to pay their respects to their beloved representative.

SHMI SKYWALKER

Shmi Skywalker loved her son very much and wanted him to have a better life than that of a slave. When he got the chance to train as a Jedi, Shmi let him go.

TIME FILE

-72	Year of birth
-78	Sold into slavery and separated from her family
-67	Sold to Pi-Lippa
-41.9	Birth of Anakin
-38	Transferred from Gardulla to Watto
-32	Anakin leaves Tatooine
-30	Places C-3PO's coverings
-27	Meets and falls in love with Cliegg Lars
-27	Cliegg buys her freedom
-27	Marries Cliegg Lars
-22	Abducted by Tusken Raiders
-22	Anakin attempts to rescue her but she dies in his arms

DID YOU KNOW?

Shmi gave C-3PO his coverings, two years after Anakin departed and before she was married.

She was 1.63 metres tall.

Shmi's body was buried next to two twin graves of Owen's forebears.

IDENTITY FILE

Shmi Skywalker was Anakin's mother. When Shmi was very young, her family was abducted by pirates who sold her into slavery.

Shmi worked extremely hard to provide Anakin with a good life, despite their status as slaves. She understood that Anakin had special abilities, and hoped that he would have a better life as a Jedi than she could offer him. Anakin was selfless, kind and gifted. His birth was extraordinary because there was no father. Some have speculated that it was the will of the Force that created Anakin in Shmi's womb.

VARIOUS MASTERS

A few of her masters showed Shmi some amount of kindness. Pi-Lippa, for example, taught her various technical skills and promised to eventually free her. Sadly, she died before she could keep her promise, and Shmi became the property of one of Pi-Lippa's relatives.

Eventually, Shmi found herself and her child, Anakin, slaves to Gardulla the Hutt on Tatooine. Gardulla subsequently lost the pair to Watto as part of a Podrace bet. Although he was cruel and rough, Watto allowed Shmi some amount of independence. When not working for him, she was allowed to clean computer memory devices in order to earn a little money.

AFTER ANAKIN

After the Jedi Knight Qui-Gon Jinn took her son away to Coruscant, a moisture farmer named Cliegg Lars fell in love with Shmi. Cliegg purchased her in order to secure her freedom. After they had married, Shmi settled with Cliegg and his family on their moisture farm outside of Mos Eisley. She loved Cliegg's son Owen as if he were her own son.

A BITTER END

One morning when Shmi was out picking mushrooms, she was viciously abducted by a band of Tusken Raiders. Some 30 local farmers formed search parties, but none were successful, and only four survived. However, having seen her fate in nightmares, Anakin found her and spoke to her before she died.

Shmi was tortured to death in an intense Tusken Raider ritual called a bloodrite.

IDENTITY FILE

Watto was a junk dealer on Tatooine. He was a Toydarian and sold a wide range of machinery. Those who bartered with him discovered that he was a shrewd merchant. His shop was a treasure trove of discarded machinery and spare parts. His keen memory allowed him to keep track of his stock, and his Toydarian mind prevented him from falling victim to Jedi mind powers. Greedy and immoral, Watto lost Anakin while betting on the Boonta Eve Podrace with Qui-Gon Jinn.

Having won Shmi and Anakin Skywalker from Gardulla the Hutt in a Podracing bet, Watto put them both to work in his shop. Young Anakin showed an incredible talent for machinery repair, and Watto took a shine to the boy. Even though he was unscrupulous enough to keep a slave, Watto was a fair master.

The boy was a prime source of income for Watto, not only in keeping his machinery running, but also by actually competing for him in the Podraces.

SMALL WINGS

BLUE SKIN

PUDGY BODY

Watto was a stout, crabby, unshaven Toydarian, with rapidly flapping wings that kept him hovering at about a metre off the ground. He had a knack for haggling and could not be affected by Jedi mind tricks.

DID YOU KNOW?

As a young Toydarian, Watto enlisted in the army of the Ossiki Confederacy. He fought in the seasonal wars of his home planet and sustained injuries that left him with a broken tusk and a lame leg.

Whenever his shop was running smoothly, Watto flew up above the shop to his nest, which recalled the muck nests of Toydaria. There he had a wall given over to his treasured collection of Podrace memorabilia, including the Grand Trophy from Ando Prime Centrum's course, a Twi'lek siren whistle, a glove once owned by the famous Podracer Bekk Tunit, a victory chain stolen from Sebulba and a Toydarian N'Omis flower.

GAMBLING DEBTS

Watto was rendered nearly destitute by his chronic gambling and was forced to sell Shmi. A moisture farmer named Cliegg Lars had fallen in love with her and purchased her freedom.

C-3PO QUIZ

An intelligent protocol droid like me has access to vast banks of data, but human beings have to reply on their memories. How complete is your knowledge of the history of the galaxy? How many facts do you remember? Complete this quiz to find out how much you have retained in your memory's data banks!

QUESTION 1

Which Podracer used the colour orange to distinguish him from the other racers?

A » ANAKIN SKYWALKER ☐
B » SEBULBA ☐
C » WATTO ☐

QUESTION 2

Who was Darth Sidious apprentice to?

A » DARTH PLAGUEIS ☐
B » DARTH TYRANUS ☐
C » DARTH MAUL ☐

QUESTION 3

Who did Qui-Gon Jinn save from being trampled by a Trade Federation MTT?

A » ANAKIN SKWALKER ☐
B » JAR JAR BINKS ☐
C » PADMÉ AMIDALA ☐

QUESTION 4

Who told Obi-Wan Kenobi about the existence of Kamino?

A » DEXTER JETTSTER ☐
B » MASTER YODA ☐
C » ZAM WESELL ☐

QUESTION 5

Of which world was Poggle the Lesser Archduke?

A » GEONOSIS ☐
B » DANTOOINE ☐
C » CORUSCANT ☐

QUESTION 6

Whose hand did Count Dooku cut off with his Lightsaber?

A » OBI-WAN KENOBI ☐
B » MACE WINDU ☐
C » ANAKIN SKYWALKER ☐

QUESTION 7

Who kidnapped Chancellor Palpatine?

A » COUNT DOOKU ☐
B » NUTE GUNRAY ☐
C » GENERAL GRIEVOUS ☐

QUESTION 8

What did Darth Sidious use to kill Mace Windu?

A » A LIGHTSABER ☐
B » SITH LIGHTNING ☐
C » FORCE CHOKE ☐

QUESTION 9

Where was Padmé Amidala buried?

A » NABOO ☐
B » CORUSCANT ☐
C » THE LARS FAMILY HOMESTEAD ON TATOOINE ☐

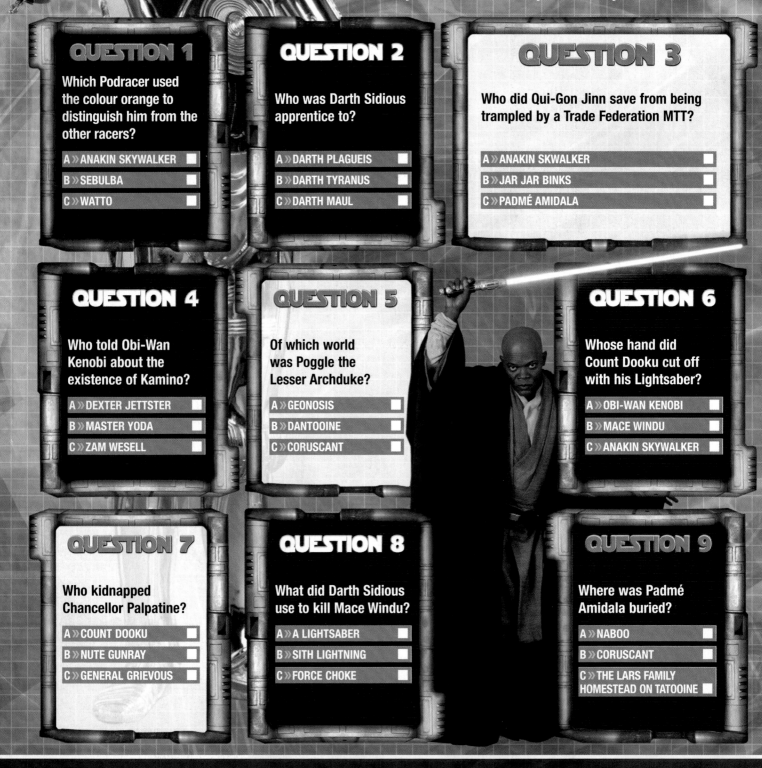

QUESTION 10

What did Luke try to persuade his uncle to let him do?

A » WORK ON THE FAMILY MOISTURE FARM ☐

B » BECOME A JEDI KNIGHT LIKE HIS FATHER BEFORE HIM ☐

C » JOIN THE ACADEMY ☐

QUESTION 11

Who did Han Solo shoot in Mos Eisley Cantina?

A » GREEDO ☐

B » PONDA BABA ☐

C » A STORMTROOPER ☐

QUESTION 12

When questioned by Grand Moff Tarkin, which planet did Princess Leia say housed the Rebel base?

A » TATOOINE ☐

B » YAVIN ☐

C » DANTOOINE ☐

QUESTION 13

Which of these did Luke not succeed in lifting as part of his Jedi training?

A » YODA ☐

B » R2-D2 ☐

C » HIS X-WING FIGHTER ☐

QUESTION 14

What did Han Solo do to keep Luke warm when they were lost in the ice on Hoth?

A » WRAPPED HIM IN A BLANKET ☐

B » PUT HIM INSIDE THE BODY OF A DEAD TAUNTAUN ☐

C » PUT HIM INSIDE THE BODY OF A DEAD WAMPA ☐

QUESTION 15

Who tracked the *Millennium Falcon* to Cloud City?

A » BOBA FETT ☐

B » DARTH VADER ☐

C » JANGO FETT ☐

QUESTION 16

What beast did Jabba the Hutt force Luke to fight?

A » HAMMERHEAD ☐

B » BANTHA ☐

C » RANCOR ☐

QUESTION 17

Who stole the plans for the second Death Star?

A » PRINCESS LEIA ☐

B » THE BOTHANS ☐

C » MON MOTHMA ☐

QUESTION 18

Who destroyed the second Death Star?

A » LANDO CALRISSIAN ☐

B » LUKE SKYWALKER ☐

C » DARTH VADER ☐

1-3 » OH MY! YOU KNOW EVEN LESS THAN R2-D2!

4-6 » YOU ARE NOWHERE NEAR THE STANDARD OF A PROTOCOL DROID.

7-10 » YOU NEED TO TRY HARDER THAN THIS IF YOU ARE GOING TO IMPRESS ME!

11-14 » FAIRLY IMPRESSIVE. YOUR CIRCUITS ARE IN GOOD WORKING ORDER … FOR A HUMAN.

15-18 » YOU MUST HAVE THE MIND OF A COMPUTER - HOW HAS A HUMAN DEVELOPED SUCH AN EXCELLENT MEMORY BANK?

ANSWERS

GIVE YOURSELF ONE POINT FOR EVERY CORRECT ANSWER.
1B » 2A » 3B » 4A » 5A » 6C » 7C » 8B » 9A » 10C » 11A » 12C » 13C » 14B » 15A » 16C » 17B » 18A

ANAKIN SKYWALKER

Anakin and Padmé travelled to Geonosis to rescue Obi-Wan. They were captured, and joined Kenobi in an execution arena. Faced with certain death, they declared their love for one another.

Anakin lived on Tatooine until he met Qui-Gon Jinn. The Jedi Master took the boy away to be trained as a Jedi, although Anakin found it difficult to leave his mother behind.

TIME FILE

-41.9	Year of birth
-32	Wins Boonta Eve Classic Podrace
-32	Freed from slavery and leaves Shmi to become a Jedi
-32	Destroys droid control ship during the Battle of Naboo
-32	Death of Qui-Gon Jinn
-29.1	Mission with Obi-Wan to Zonama Sekot
-29	Builds his lightsaber on Ilum
-22	Mission with Obi-Wan to Ansion
-22	Assigned to protect Padmé Amidala
-22	Declares his love for Padmé at the Lake Country on Naboo
-22	Returns to Tatooine to save Shmi, but she dies in his arms
-22	Goes to Geonosis to rescue Obi-Wan Kenobi
-22	Battle of Geonosis
-22	Loses arm during duel with Count Dooku
-22	Marries Padmé Amidala
-20	Battle of Jabiim
-20	Becomes a Jedi Knight

-19.5	Last sees Padmé before embarking on the Outer Rim Sieges
-19	Rescues Chancellor Palpatine from Grievous
-19	Learns Padmé is pregnant but has nightmare of her death during childbirth
-19	Learns Palpatine is a Sith Lord
-19	Sides with Palpatine after Mace Windu attempts to arrest the Chancellor
-19	Palpatine gives Anakin the name Darth Vader
-19	Attacks the Jedi Temple during Order 66
-19	Goes to Mustafar to wipe out the Separatist leaders
-19	Padmé confronts him about the attack on the Jedi Temple
-19	Mortally wounded during a duel with Obi-Wan on Mustafar
-19	Palpatine brings Anakin back to Coruscant where Anakin is placed in life-supporting armor
-19	Learns of Padmé's death

IDENTITY FILE

Anakin Skywalker was born a slave, but his mother always knew that there was something special about him. Strongly attuned to the Force, Anakin had the ability to sense events before they happened. He was not only resourceful, intuitive and competitive, but also loving and kind. He had no father and was possibly conceived by the will of the Force itself.

Anakin Skywalker left an indelible mark on the history of the galaxy, leading it through periods of lightness and dark. He would go on to become one of the most legendary figures in the galaxy and, as the prophesied Chosen One, to ultimately bring balance to the Force.

THE DARK SIDE

When Anakin accused the Chancellor of being a Sith Lord, Palpatine did not deny it. He offered Anakin the knowledge and power of the dark side, promising a path to the Force that had no rules, no code and no boundaries. Anakin reported the Chancellor to Mace Windu, but then realised that Palpatine could be his only chance to save Padmé. He stopped Windu killing the Sith Lord by chopping off his arm. Palpatine, revealed as Darth Sidious, killed Windu with a massive burst of Sith lightning. Anakin had now committed himself to the dark path. He knelt before Darth Sidious, proclaiming himself to be a servant of the Sith. Sidious granted Anakin a Sith name: Darth Vader. He then sent Vader to wipe out the Jedi at the Jedi Temple. On that terrible night, Darth Vader became the scourge of the Jedi. He killed all those he could find, including younglings, his eyes burning yellow with Sith intensity. Anakin Skywalker was no more.

A FLAWED PADAWAN

Anakin grew into a confident, headstrong young man with an impulsive nature and a flair for adventure. He was in love with the beautiful Padmé Amidala and his feelings challenged his Jedi vows. A darker side emerged within Anakin, which he found difficult to control. Anakin began to feel that his Master, Obi-Wan Kenobi, was holding him back.

THE CLONE WARS

Anakin found the Clone Wars invigorating. He felt *alive* in combat, and his incredible Force abilities were further honed. Time and again, Anakin felt restrained by his oaths to the Jedi. He couldn't share his darker thoughts with his fellow Jedi, but he knew that such a path was a gateway to more power. The only friend he could confide in was Chancellor Palpatine.

PADMÉ AMIDALA

Disregarding the Jedi code, Anakin and Padmé were secretly married in a ceremony on Naboo. It was another step towards Anakin's eventual destruction.

DARK VISIONS

When Padmé became pregnant. Anakin was plagued with prophetic nightmares that she would die in childbirth. Palpatine told Anakin that the Sith Lord Darth Plagueis the Wise could coax life out of midi-chlorians, either to create new life or to prevent death. This was the promised power of the Sith. Anakin, who had been searching for a way to prevent Padmé from dying, listened intently.

General Grievous called Anakin the 'hero with no fear'.

SEBULBA

Sebulba was an excellent showman and many race fans loved him despite his unsportsmanlike conduct. After all, they were often guaranteed a great crash if Sebulba was in the running.

IDENTITY FILE

An especially dangerous Dug who could once be found roaming the streets of Mos Espa, Sebulba was a shifty Podracing champion who never allowed rules and sportsmanship to get in the way of victory. His homeworld was Malastare, and he was the reigning champion of the Outer Rim Podrace circuit in the waning days of the Republic. His orange vehicle, a Collor Pondrat Plug-F Mammoth Podracer, was souped-up and overpowered.

Sebulba was a hotshot with an inflated ego. Among his most prized possessions were a lovely pair of Twi'lek masseuses who rubbed him down before a stressful race.

AN UNDERHANDED WINNER

Many of Sebulba's victories were won through the use of illegal weaponry hidden aboard his vehicle. He flew dirty, and would even stoop to sabotaging a competitor's Podracer before a race began.

A TALENTED SLAVE BOY

Sebulba was heavily favoured to win the Boonta Eve Classic. In a surprising upset, however, a local slave boy backed by a mysterious outlander bested him in the contest. To add even more insult to this career-injury, Sebulba lost control of his Podracer in the final stretch, and crashed the expensive giant into the desert sands.

OVERCOMING DEFEAT

Sebulba was not embarrassed for long. He quickly bounced back from his defeat by purchasing the very Podracer that bested him. Sebulba bought the Radon-Ulzer from Qui-Gon Jinn and repainted it with his distinctive orange racing colour. He won the Vinta Harvest Classic on Malastare shortly afterwards. Sebulba's son, Hekula, inherited the Radon-Ulzer Podracer.

PODRACING

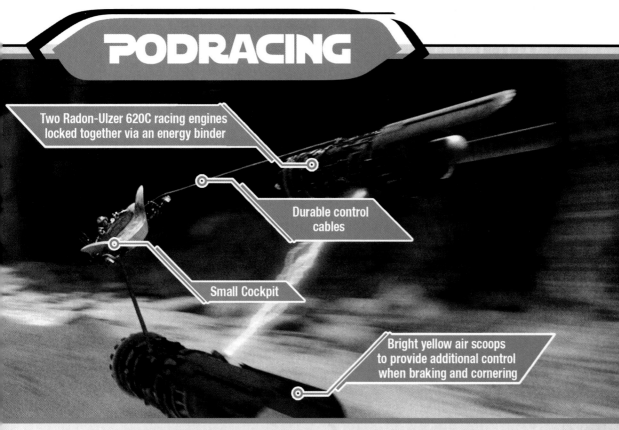

Two Radon-Ulzer 620C racing engines locked together via an energy binder

Durable control cables

Small Cockpit

Bright yellow air scoops to provide additional control when braking and cornering

Built in secret by Anakin Skywalker, his shiny blue and silver Podracer was boasted to be the fastest ever to compete in the Boonta Eve Classic.

IDENTITY FILE

Podracing was a high-speed sport that could trace its origins to ancient contests of animal-drawn chariots. Long ago, a foolhardy mechanic named Phoebos revisited the chariot design, replacing the cart with a repulsorlift Pod and the beasts of burden with rocket jet engines. A new and dangerous spectacle was created.

In the waning years of the Republic, when prohibitive laws failed to extend to the Outer Rim Territories, Podracing was still quite successful despite being banned in the central systems.

The Boonta Eve Classic was the largest annual Podrace held on Tatooine and it started in the Mos Espa Gand Arena. Thousands of spectators would congregate to watch.

THE BOONTA EVE CLASSIC

The Mos Espa course blazed out of the arena onto the Starlite Flats, an easy stretch of desert where aggressive Podracers jockeyed for strong starting positions.

The racers had to line up in single file to enter the curving canyon that cut through the Waldo Flats. This opened up into Mushroom Mesa, a rocky expanse dominated by immense bulbous rock formations.

Metta Drop, a sudden escarpment, dropped the racers onto Ebe Crater Valley, where they again had to navigate a narrow opening (the Notch) to enter Beggar's Canyon.

The race continued onto a length of desert plains abutting the Dune Sea. Arch Canyon forced pilots to manoeuvre through stone wickets before entering another series of canyons. Emerging from the caves, the pilots careened through the tight Canyon Dune Turn, known to be a campsite for vengeful Tusken Raiders.

Podracers that survived potshots from the Sand People then had to dodge the rocky obstacles in Bindy Bend before entering the last stretch of canyon, which included the Coil, Jett's Chute and the Corkscrew.

Exiting the Corkscrew via the Devil's Doorknob, the pilots emerged onto the Hutt Flats, a broad featureless expanse that led back to the arena. This entire circuit represented one lap, and the Boonta Eve Classic required three laps for completion.

FAMOUS PODRACING TRACKS

The Boonta Classic was the most popular Podrace and had the highest mortality rate.

The frigid planet of Ando Prime featured an icy racecourse sponsored by the Bendu monks.

The watery world of Aquilaris had a track that cut through the sinking relic of the Old City.

The gaseous planet Ord Ibanna had a foolhardy course that spanned the connecting bridges and pipelines of floating mining platforms.

Tropical Baroonda let Podracers scream through the swamp world's ancient ruins.

The industrial wasteland world of Mon Gazza opened up its spice mines for races.

Perhaps the world best known for Podracing was Malastare, whose methane lakes and mountain ranges hosted such notable courses as the Malastare 100 and the Vinta Harvest Classic.

Podracing has seen a decline in recent years, and many of the galaxy's most famous tracks are now vacant or have been converted to other amusements for a fickle crowd.

C-3PO (SEE-THREEPIO)

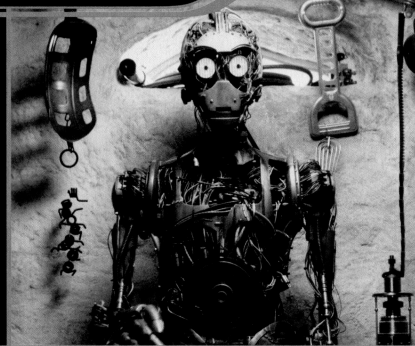

ROUGH BEGINNINGS

Threepio was built by Anakin Skywalker and constructed from reclaimed parts. He was programmed with a detailed knowledge of over 5000 droids. He was also fluent in several million forms of communication and could even converse with Tusken Raiders and Jawas. Although unfinished and little more than a collection of wires and circuitry, Threepio served the Skywalkers faithfully.

Anakin Skywalker spent many long hours in Watto's junkyard scavenging for parts to build C-3PO. The droid's recycled structural framework was over 80 years old, but other components were built by Anakin himself. The original droid frame used as Threepio's foundation had damaged photoreceptors, which Anakin replaced with the eyes from a used droid in Watto's shop. Although C-3PO was largely complete, Anakin was unable to give him a 'skin' because droid plating was extremely expensive.

Two years after her son's departure to become a Jedi, Shmi Skywalker acquired a set of old droid plating from her then master, Watto. Shmi installed the plates to help the droid last longer in the sandy environment.

C-3PO was constructed on Tatooine. From such humble beginnings, no one could have guessed that he would one day play a central role in the future of the galaxy.

LOYAL SERVANT

C-3PO stayed with Shmi when she married Cliegg Lars and moved to the Lars family moisture farm near Mos Eisley. When Anakin and Padmé Amidala returned to Tatooine, they were greeted by a complete, albeit mismatched C-3PO. He joined Anakin, Padmé and his new counterpart R2-D2 on a rescue mission to save their friend Obi-Wan Kenobi.

As part of the Rebel Alliance, C-3PO had many adventures that he could never have anticipated, including being mistaken for a god by the Ewoks.

THE CLONE WARS

During the Clone Wars Threepio served his mistress, Padmé Amidala, faithfully, yet often found himself helpless against the turmoil around him as the Republic dissolved into the Galactic Empire. After the Jedi attempt to arrest Palpatine, C-3PO heard a rumour that they were going to banish all droids. He went with Padmé to Mustafar and brought her back to her ship when she was injured by her husband.

AN ODD COUPLE

Threepio seemed to talk down to Artoo or argue with him more often than not. And Artoo, with his own agenda, could send his companion into a state of high dudgeon. Despite their constant disagreements, the droids were really best friends in every sense and depended on each other to survive in an often harsh galaxy.

"DON'T BLAME ME. I'M JUST AN INTERPRETER. I'M NOT SUPPOSED TO KNOW A POWER SOCKET FROM A COMPUTER TERMINAL."

C-3PO was loyal to the Skywalker family and remained at Padmé Amidala's side whether times were good or bad. He was a witness when she married her true love, Anakin Skywalker. He was there when Anakin turned to the dark side and threw Padmé to the ground as if dead.

IN ROYAL SERVICE

Many years after the destruction of the Republic, the droids were in the service of the Royal House of Alderaan. They were eventually put aboard the *Tantive IV* while it was on a secret mission to intercept stolen Imperial data. They were both given override orders that restricted all references to Princess Leia's presence aboard the ship. In Threepio's case, this activated a total memory block regarding the princess.

When Imperial forces boarded the ship, Threepio followed Artoo, who was carrying the stolen Death Star plans, into an escape pod that landed on Tatooine. Both were captured by Jawas, who sold them to young Skywalker's uncle, Owen Lars.

REBEL DROID

C-3PO remained faithful to the Skywalker family. After Luke's family was killed under Darth Vader's orders, Threepio escaped with Luke, R2-D2 and Obi-Wan Kenobi. Thus began an exciting and dangerous set of adventures that would put Threepio into the history books as an integral part of the Rebellion.

His pivotal role in reuniting the Skywalker twins bridged two generations and helped to bring about the Rebellion's first crushing blow against the evil Empire.

IDENTITY FILE

C-3PO was a worrisome protocol droid who made up half of the most famous robot team in the galaxy. Along with his squat companion R2-D2, C-3PO had enough adventures to fill several lives. C-3PO was a little stiff and awkward in his manner and often overly negative in his outlook. Nevertheless, he played a key role in many of the important events of galactic history.

R2-D2 (ARTOO-DETOO)

R2-D2 aided Luke on countless missions, joining the young Jedi at the Battle of Yavin and on his perilous trips to Dagobah and Bespin.

IDENTITY FILE

A bold and spirited astromech droid, Artoo was one of the most famous automatons in the galaxy. He was designed to operate in deep space, interfacing with fighter craft and computer systems in order to augment the capabilities of ships and their pilots. He was usually placed in a socket behind the cockpit, where he monitored and diagnosed flight performance, mapped and stored hyperspace data, and pinpointed technical errors or faulty computer coding. He was well versed in starship repair for hundreds of styles of spacecraft and could exist in the vacuum of space indefinitely.

Artoo conversed in an information-dense electronic language that sounded to the untrained ear like beeps, boops, chirps and whistles. Although he could understand most forms of human speech, Artoo's own communications had to be interpreted by Threepio or by ship computers to which he sent electronic data.

THREEPIO

Artoo developed an odd relationship with Threepio over the years. The protocol droid behaved like a fussy mother hen, almost constantly cajoling, belittling or arguing with his squat counterpart. Artoo was loyal, inventive and sarcastic. Although he always seemed to want to aggravate Threepio, they had deep mutual respect and trust for each other.

EVER FAITHFUL

Artoo was an astromech droid assigned to Queen Amidala's Royal Starship. When the vessel was damaged by enemy fire, he valiantly repaired the damaged deflector shield generator.

Artoo accompanied Anakin Skywalker and Senator Amidala on their retreat to Naboo and their detour to Tatooine, where he was reunited with his counterpart C-3PO. Aboard Amidala's vessel, Artoo received and played a message from Obi-Wan Kenobi linking the assassination attempt on the Senator with the expanding Separatist movement.

They all went to Geonosis, and as Padmé and Anakin wandered into a dangerous Geonosian droid factory, Artoo and Threepio followed. Artoo again came to the rescue, using his antigrav boosters to fly to Amidala's aid and his computer interface to stop a deadly downpour of molten metal from killing the Senator. He even helped reassemble C-3PO after a decapitating tangle with droid factory machinery.

LAST MISSION WITH ANAKIN

In the final days of the Republic, R2-D2 was assigned to serve Jedi Knight Anakin Skywalker in the Clone Wars. Seated in the droid socket of Anakin's Jedi starfighter, R2-D2 accompanied his master and Obi-Wan Kenobi on their mission to rescue Chancellor Palpatine from the clutches of General Grievous, and his ingenuity and spirit proved invaluable once again. As the Republic crumbled and the evil Galactic Empire rose from its ashes, the little droid accompanied Anakin on one fateful last mission to the volcanic planet of Mustafar.

THE END OF THE JEDI

After Anakin was beaten by Obi-Wan on Mustafar, Artoo helped to take Padmé Amidala to medical help, but she died as the Republic crashed around them. When Obi-Wan and Yoda were forced into hiding, the tiny droid and C-3PO were given to a new master as they began a journey that would involve them deeply in the Rebel cause.

Artoo's fully rotational domed head contained infrared receptors, electromagnetic-field sensors, a register readout and logic dispenser, dedicated energy receptors, a radar eye, heat and motion detectors and a holographic recorder and projector.

Two treaded legs provided the droid with mobility, and a third leg could drop down for extra stability on rough terrain. Artoo also has flotation devices and a periscoping visual scanner to guide him while submerged.

Behind doors in his cylindrical body lie hidden instruments, including a storage/retrieval jack for computer linkup, auditory receivers, flame-retardant foam dispenser, electric shock prod, high-powered spotlight, grasping claw, laser welder, circular saw and a Cybot acoustic signaller.

A BRAVE DROID

Many years later, Artoo was aboard the *Tantive IV* when it was caught by the Imperial Star Destroyer *Devastator*. Princess Leia Organa placed stolen data plans for an Imperial super weapon into R2-D2 and told him to take them to Obi-Wan Kenobi somewhere in the Tatooine desert. The droid met Luke Skywalker, the son of his former master, and became deeply involved in the Galactic Civil War.

R2-D2 rode with Skywalker when Luke fired the famous shot that destroyed the first Death Star. The droid was hit by a laser blast in the process, and when Skywalker visited swampy Dagobah to start his Jedi training with Master Yoda, Artoo suffered a few indignities at Yoda's hands. The droid also played a prominent role in the rescue of Han Solo from the palace of Jabba the Hutt, hiding Skywalker's lightsaber until it was needed.

The inquisitive little droid was programmed for navigation and repair, but he was also capable of independent thought and his quick thinking saved his friends numerous times.

COUNT DOOKU

Whipped into a state of passion, Skywalker ended Dooku's life, playing further into the hands of the evil Palpatine.

IDENTITY FILE

Count Dooku was a powerful leader and a master swordsman. Once a prominent Jedi, he became disillusioned with the Republic and felt that the Jedi betrayed themselves by serving the politicians. Dooku abandoned the Jedi Order and disappeared for nearly ten years before emerging as leader of the Separatist movement. He appeared to be a frail, elderly man, but he was in fact a disciple of the dark side and a fierce warrior. Secretly, he was also Darth Tyranus, a Sith Lord and Apprentice to the mysterious Darth Sidious.

JEDI BEGINNINGS

At the age of 13, Dooku was chosen to be the Padawan of Thame Cerulian. At the time, Lorian Nod was his best friend at the Jedi Temple. When Nod tried to blame Dooku for stealing a Sith Holocron, Nod was expelled from the Jedi Temple and Dooku learned not to believe in friendship.

Dooku never fully gave the Order his inmost allegiance. He maintained a streak of independence, which he transmitted to his pupils, including the late Qui-Gon Jinn. Dooku's considerable strength in the Force made him enigmatic even to Yoda, and the Council underestimated Dooku's interest in power. He left the Jedi Order after the Battle of Naboo, returning to his homeworld of Serenno and reclaiming his family title of Count.

The elegant and accomplished Count Dooku had once been a Jedi Master, but he turned towards the dark side of the Force and became Apprentice to the wicked Darth Sidious. He was a man of deadly cunning and excellent swordsmanship.

TIME FILE

-78	Year of birth
-67	Chosen as Thane Cerulean's Padawan
-78	Takes Qui-Gon as a Padawan
-67	Qui-Gon becomes a Jedi Knight
-67	Becomes a Jedi Master
-50	Takes Komari Vosa as a Padawan
-41	Battle of Galidraan
-32	Death of Qui-Gon Jinn
-32	Obtains his solar sailer
-32	Goes into exile and establishes a hidden base
-32	Changes crystal in his lightsaber to emit a red blade
-31.5	Hires Jango Fett
-24	Reemerges as leader of the Separatists
-22	Battle of Geonosis
-22	Dark Reaper Project
-19	Killed during a duel with Anakin Skywalker above Coruscant

THE SITH AND THE LURE OF THE DARK SIDE

It was a great blow to the Jedi order when Count Dooku voluntarily renounced his commission. A strong-minded man, Dooku's ideas were often out of step with those of the Jedi Council. His challenging views were often echoed by his former Padawan, Qui-Gon Jinn.

After his departure, he disappeared for years, re-emerging as a political firebrand fanning the flames of rebellion in the galaxy. In an alarmingly short time, Dooku rallied thousands of systems to his cause, building a growing Separatist movement that threatened to split the Republic.

Behind a veneer of elegance and well-tabled political arguments, Dooku had been corrupted by the power of the dark side. Dooku was seduced to the dark side by Darth Sidious, the Dark Lord of the Sith. Dooku adopted the name Darth Tyranus.

SEPARATIST LEADER AND WARMONGER

Under Dooku's leadership, several hundred solar systems declared their intentions to secede from the Republic. As Tyranus, he contacted the notorious bounty hunter Jango Fett to become the template for a hidden clone army on Kamino. As Dooku, he appealed to the greed of the galaxy's most powerful commerce barons to consolidate their forces to challenge the Republic.

Deep within the mighty spires of Geonosis, Dooku chaired a meeting to formally create the Confederacy of Independent Systems. Separatist Senators alongside representatives from the Commerce Guild, the Trade Federation, the Corporate Alliance, the InterGalactic Banking Clan and the Techno Union pooled their resources together to form the largest military force in the galaxy. The Separatists were ready for war.

Obi-Wan Kenobi and Jedi reinforcements arrived. The droid armies of the Separatists battled with the Republic's clone army. Dooku escaped, with the Jedi aware of his succumbing to the dark side, but yet still unaware of his Sith allegiance. He met with his master, Darth Sidious, and delivered the good news. The Clone Wars had begun.

TREACHERY AND DEATH

Ultimately, Dooku was betrayed by the man who had mentored him. Palpatine, who was also Darth Sidious, encouraged young Anakin Skywalker to execute Dooku.

THE SEPARATISTS

Brought together by Count Dooku, the Separatists wanted to destroy the Republic and introduce a more capitalist system that would benefit them and help make them more money.

TRADE FEDERATION

The Trade Federation was a consortium of merchants and transportation providers that controlled shipping throughout the galaxy. Under the rule of the scheming Neimoidians, it had full representation in the Galactic Senate, as if it were a member world. In order to rein in the Trade Federation, as well as raise funds for an overburdened government, the Republic approved the taxation of outlying trade routes.

Outraged, the Trade Federation blockaded the peaceful planet of Naboo in protest. Its fleet of massive battleships surrounded the pastoral world, cutting off direly needed supplies to the planet.

What no one in the galaxy knew was that the Trade Federation was just a pawn in a much larger game. The Trade Federation's leaders had allied themselves with a mysterious Sith Lord, Darth Sidious. Egged on by him, the normally cowardly Neimoidians began a full-scale invasion of Naboo.

By banding together, the people of Naboo were able to overthrow their oppressors and the leaders were arrested. The Neimoidians, however, kept Darth Sidious' existence a secret.

Even after the Senate's reprimands for the Naboo incident, the Trade Federation nonetheless continued to operate. Nute Gunray allied himself to Count Dooku and was willing to pledge the forces of the Trade Federation to the Confederacy of Independent Systems on one condition: the death of Padmé Amidala. The young Naboo politician became the target of several assassination attempts, but she escaped time and again. Nonetheless, Gunray committed the Trade Federation to the Separatist cause, and in the first battle of the Clone Wars, the Trade Federation droid army fought against the clone army of the Republic.

POGGLE THE LESSER

IDENTITY FILE

Poggle the Lesser was the Archduke of Geonosis and played a key role in the Separatist movement. He lived within the rocky spires of Geonosis and oversaw the production of battle droids. Poggle was power-hungry and ruthless. He was eventually killed by Darth Vader when Darth Sidious had no more need for the Separatists.

Poggle was born into a low caste in a society where position was very important. However, he overturned the strict traditions of the Geonosians and aspired to leadership.

HEARTLESS AMBITION

He had first tried to topple the regime of the previous leader, Hadiss the Vaulted, with the help of a mutinous brigade of dissidents. They were all rounded up and sentenced to death. However, although many of his followers died, Poggle had the secret backing of Darth Sidious, who provided much-needed resources for his rebellion. Just a year later, Poggle oversaw the death of Hadiss in the execution arena.

After purging the Geonosian ranks of any rebels, Poggle became Archduke of Geonosis. His ruthlessness was legendary – the longbone he used as a command staff was rumoured to be the remains of one of the many political opponents he murdered.

THE BATTLE OF GEONOSIS

Indebted to Darth Sidious, Poggle committed himself and his workers to the growing Separatist cause. He increased production in the Geonosian foundries in order to build up armies for the Sith Lord.

When Obi-Wan Kenobi, Padmé Amidala and Anakin Skywalker were discovered spying on Geonosis, Poggle sentenced them to execution. The Senator and the two Jedi were tied up in the execution arena, but they escaped and put up a powerful fight against the vicious beasts that had been set on them. The sudden arrival of Jedi reinforcements turned the public spectacle into a frenzied battle.

Poggle and the other Separatist leaders retreated into an underground command centre. They watched in shock and dread as Republican forces arrived with their newly formed clone army. Poggle ordered his warriors to withdraw into the catacombs.

THE ULTIMATE WEAPON

Poggle had been hiding top-secret plans for an ultimate weapon that the Geonosians were contracted to construct. He returned the blueprints to Count Dooku, who escaped to take the plans to his Sith Master.

NUTE GUNRAY

Remaining viceroy of the Trade Federation, Nute Gunray survived several hearings and four trials in the Supreme Court.

IDENTITY FILE

Viceroy Nute Gunray's home planet was Neimoidia. The Neimoidians were known for their outstanding business and organisational skills, but Gunray was more cutthroat than most. His cunning and lack of scruples helped him to attain the position of Viceroy of the Trade Federation. Gunray would do anything that would benefit him financially, careless of the cost to workers or the effect on the environment. He left many planets as barren, dead balls, floating in space.

JUSTICE FAILS

Gunray led the blockade and invasion of the planet of Naboo, under the orders of the mysterious Darth Sidious. Gunray tried to force Queen Amidala to sign a treaty that would legitimise his occupation of Naboo. He arrogantly set himself up in her throne room, taunting the planet's governor, Sio Bibble.

Darth Vader was sent by Darth Sidious to kill Gunray. The Neimoidian pleaded for mercy, but Vader silenced him with a slashing blade through his torso.

TRUE COLOURS

Gunray's cowardly true colours showed themselves when Naboo freedom fighters stormed the Royal Palace. He cowered behind his battle droids, afraid for his life. Queen Amidala broke into her own palace and blasted through Gunray's protectors. At gunpoint, Amidala declared the occupation over.

CORRUPT JUSTICE

Gunray and his lieutenant Rune Haako were arrested by Republic officials and taken to answer for their crimes. They risked losing their lucrative trade franchise from this illegal siege.

But even justice could be bought in the final years of the Republic. After four trials in the Supreme Court, Gunray kept his position of Viceroy.

The courts ordered the Trade Federation to reduce its armies, and banned them from ever expanding them again. However, there were many rumours that the Trade Federation had retained a secret military.

THE CLONE WARS

When Count Dooku's Separatist movement began tearing apart the Republic, Gunray liked the idea of galactic reforms that would benefit commerce. He allied himself with the Confederacy of Independent Systems, on the condition that Padmé Amidala would be assassinated. Padmé was now Senator of Naboo, and Gunray wanted her removed.

The bounty hunter Jango Fett recruited Zam Wesell to kill the Senator of Naboo. Wesell failed, but Padmé was captured by Separatist forces and was to be executed before Gunray. However, the Jedi Knights arrived just in time with clone troopers. When the shooting started, Gunray turned coward and fled the conflict.

DEATH AND BETRAYAL

When Sidious moved the Separatist leadership to Mustafar, the end of the war was near and so was the end of Gunray. Darth Sidious no longer needed the Separatists, who he had just been using to help him become Emperor of the galaxy. Darth Vader was sent to destroy the terrified separatists; Gunray watched, snivelling, as Vader's Lightsaber sliced through the barons, knowing that it would soon be his turn to die.

BOUNTY HUNTERS

BOUNTY HUNTERS

Bounty hunters were independent law enforcers who could be hired by anyone for the right price. They were well armed and well trained, and they were prepared to track down anyone with a price on their head.

Although by nature bounty hunters operated in the shadows and the gutters of society, many were sanctioned law enforcers. This allowed them to carry all sorts of weaponry unavailable to the general public.

Many hunters worked for the Bounty Hunters Guild, an organisation that provided supplies, aid and the latest warrants for the pickings.

GREEDO

The Rodian bounty hunter Greedo was hired by Jabba the Hutt to kill and collect on Han Solo. He had a tapir-like snout, bulbous eyes, pea-green skin and a crest of spines on top of his skull.

Greedo finally challenged Solo in the Mos Eisley Cantina. At blaster point, Greedo demanded that Solo pay his debt to Jabba. When Solo claimed he didn't have the money with him, Greedo lost his patience. He opened fire but his shot missed, allowing Solo the chance to kill him. Solo fired his blaster pistol and ripped through a table and the Rodian's chest.

Greedo's corpse was collected by the bartender. His powerful pheromones were used to create a very special drink for Jabba the Hutt. Greedo was survived by a relative named Beedo, who took his place in Jabba's court.

AURRA SING

Aurra Sing was a humanoid alien with chalk-white skin and long, blood-letting fingers. She was raised on the mean streets of Nar Shaddaa's vertical cities and her mother was a spice-addled reprobate named Aunuanna. Her species was unknown. Surgically attached to her skull was a long, thin sensor implant that aided her in her hunts. She always wore a red jumpsuit and little armour.

Aurra's Force-potential was discovered when she was an infant. The mysterious Jedi known as the Dark Woman took custody of her, spiriting her away to Coruscant to begin her initiation into the Jedi way, taking her far from the dark decay of the Smuggler's Moon.

However, pain, death and vengeance had been constants in Aurra Sing's life. If her early upbringing had been happier, she might have grown to be one of the greatest of the Jedi Order. Instead, she became one its deadliest scourges. She and many other bounty hunters shared a common hatred of the Jedi.

ZAM WESELL

Although exotic and mysterious, Zam Wesell was a refined, unrelenting assassin and an excellent tracker. She kept her face hidden beneath a veil and appeared to be a beautiful human female, but she was actually a Clawdite changeling, which meant that she could change her appearance at will.

Wesell had a reputation for unsurpassed marksmanship and she was hired by Jango Fett to eliminate Senator Amidala. However, she got more than she bargained for when her assassination attempt was foiled by the Senator's Jedi protectors, who pursued her on a harrowing chase through the Coruscant skyline. She was finally killed by Jango Fett to stop her from betraying him.

DENGAR

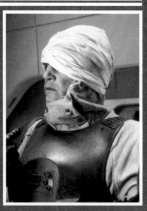

Dengar was known as 'Payback', because personal vendettas fuelled much of his career. The Corellian had been a daring swoop-racer until a competitive rival named Han Solo cut his career short. Although it was Dengar who was at fault, he blamed Han for his devastating head injury and for ruining his life.

Dengar was patched together by Imperial agents and transformed into a remorseless killer. When word of the hefty bounty on Han Solo reached him, Dengar could hardly wait to track down the smuggler.

BOSSK

Bossk was a reptilian humanoid from Trandosha, and a skilled bounty hunter. Like all Trandoshans, he had a strong build and regenerative abilities that could regrow lost limbs. He worshipped a god known as the Scorekeeper, who rewarded successful hunts in the afterlife.

Bossk was the son of Cradossk, a respected hunter and the former head of the Bounty Hunters Guild. Bossk betrayed, killed and ate his father to gain his power, but he could not hold on to it. While Bossk was leader, the Bounty Hunters Guild split into two warring factions - Bossk's Guild Reform Committee and the True Guild backed by Cradossk loyalists.

ZUCKUSS

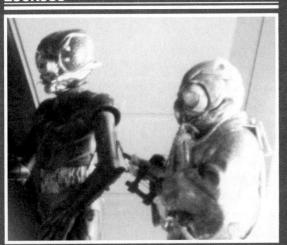

Zuckuss was a short, stocky being with a grubby robe and breather tanks attached to his head. He was one of the six bounty hunters that answered Darth Vader's call to find the *Millennium Falcon* after the Battle of Hoth.

While employed by Jabba the Hutt, Zuckuss was teamed with the analytical protocol droid bounty hunter 4-LOM. Their teamwork was impressive, as Zuckuss' instinctive style was perfectly complemented by 4-LOM's hard-edged logic.

4-LOM

Like his partner Zuckuss, the protocol droid 4-LOM answered the call sent out by Darth Vader to capture the *Millennium Falcon*. He was a humanoid droid, and his once-gleaming matte-black coverings were scarred and pitted.

4-LOM began his electronic life as a cabin steward aboard a luxury liner. A programming glitch led to antisocial behaviour, and the droid began stealing valuables from the liner's passengers.

This thievery grew and attracted the attention of Jabba the Hutt. Jabba gave 4-LOM combat computer systems and the capacity to harm sentients. When Jabba teamed him with Zuckuss, the two made a formidable team.

IG-88

IG-88 was a tall, spindly humanoid droid loaded with concealed weaponry, including a deadly gas dispenser, a flamethrower, a sonic stunner, a pulse cannon and a neural inhibitor projectile launcher.

He was developed by scientists at Holowan Laboratories. They were bursting with excitement when they activated the new generation of combat droid, but within seconds IG-88 achieved sentience and ran amok, slaughtering the hapless scientists.

IG-88 activated and downloaded his consciousness into three mechanical clones, and was thus able to spread his brand of mayhem across the galaxy. The four mechanicals IG-88A, B, C and D shared a cold, calculating consciousness bent on destruction.

IG-88 responded to Darth Vader's call to capture the *Millennium Falcon* during the events surrounding the Battle of Hoth. By this time, IG-88B had already killed over 150 beings and had a 'dismantle-on-sight' warrant in over 40 systems.

LAMA SU AND THE KAMINOANS

Lama Su was a privacy-loving Kaminoan who took great pride in the clone facility he ran. He did not know that the building of the clone army was just one part of an evil Sith plot to control the galaxy.

IDENTITY FILE

Lama Su was the Prime Minister of the remote planet Kamino, which was sea-covered and constantly ravaged by storms. Although Kaminoans preferred living in isolation, sometimes business required that they mix with other races. As the head of the ruling council of Kamino colony governors, Lama Su was one of the few Kaminoans to deal directly with outlanders.

THE PLANET KAMINO

All evidence of the world of Kamino was erased from the Jedi Archives in order to hide all evidence of the clone army. It was a lonely world beyond the Outer Rim and just south of the Rishi Maze. No one could have guessed that Kamino would play a key role in the changing times of the last days of the Republic.

Kamino was a world of unsettled oceans and never-ending storms. Global warming had melted huge shelves of inland continental ice and its oceans had swelled, covering the land and forcing the Kaminoans to adapt. Its cities were mounted on stilts to keep them safe from the churning waters below. They were enormously strong, built to resist the storms that battered them without pause.

Kamino's most prized export and best-kept secret was clones. The Kaminoans had the reputation (among those in the know) of being the best cloners in the galaxy. They traded their advanced cloning knowledge for vital raw materials needed by their waterlogged world.

THE CLONE ARMY

When a mysterious Jedi Master called Sifo-Dyas commissioned a clone army of thousands of troops, Lama Su was happy to oblige. He never questioned the role of the army or its eventual use in the Clone Wars.

Lama Su took pride in using and developing the skills of his employees. He recognised that their cloning skills were vital to Kamino's economy, and he even gave Obi-Wan Kenobi a personal tour of the cloning facility. His unfamiliarity with human behaviour (and his eagerness to impress his client) caused him to overlook Obi-Wan's ignorance of the cloning project.

Tipoca City stood on stilts in one of Kamino's raging oceans. Because of a change in environmental conditions, it was always stormy and rainy on the planet.

DID YOU KNOW?

To supply the Grand Army of the Republic with armour and transport, the Kaminoans partnered with the neighbouring Rothana system to develop advanced combat machinery.

WAR ZONE

Because of its partnership with the Galactic Republic, Kamino was repeatedly attacked by the Separatists in the early stages of the Clone Wars. However, as time went on, the Republic was starting to move its cloning operations elsewhere. The Kaminoans lost their grip on the secrecy they valued so highly, and Republic cloners began carrying out their techniques offworld.

IMPERIAL CONTROL

The Empire maintained a strong presence on Kamino to keep the planet's valuable technology from falling into the wrong hands. Some Kaminoans secretly formed a liberation army of Kamino-loyal clones who would oppose the Empire. The resultant clone uprising, which occurred a decade into the Empire's rule, was put down by the elite 501st Legion of stormtroopers. Darth Vader hired Boba Fett to lead the troopers in battle, despite the fact that Fett was himself a product of the Kaminoan hatcheries.

JANGO FETT

The first battle of the Clone Wars was fought on the dusty world of Geonosis. Although Jango fought with all his skill and courage, there was one Jedi who he could not defeat.

TIME FILE

-78	Year of birth
-67	Meets Jaster Mereel following the death of his parents
-78	Begins fighting alongside the Mandalorians
-67	Death of Jaster Mereel at Korda IV
-44	Mandalorians are wiped out by Jedi led by Dooku at Galidraan
-44	Takes prisoner and becomes a slave
-41	Escapes and becomes a bounty hunter
-31.5	Acquires *Slave I*
-31.5	Meets Zam Wesell
-31.5	Hired by Dooku for a clone army
-31.5	'Birth' of Boba Fett
-23	Meets Bossk
-22	Kills Zam Wesell on Coruscant.
-22	Flees after Obi-Wan discovers him on Kamino
-22	Pursued by Obi-Wan through the Geonosis asteroid field
-22	Killed in a duel with Mace Windu during the Battle of Geonosis

IDENTITY FILE

Jango Fett was a resourceful and dangerous bounty hunter who was known and feared throughout the galaxy. He had the reputation of being the best bounty hunter in the galaxy.

He was the son of farmers, but brutal marauders made him an orphan at an early age. At the age of ten, he was picked up by Journeyman Protector Jaster Mereel, who introduced him to life as a mercenary. Jango was raised among great warriors, who taught him how to survive in the rugged frontiers.

Fett's scarred face was concealed by the helmet of his sleek armoured suit. He was more than equipped to defend himself, with retractable wrist blades, dual pistols, a snare and other concealed weapons. His jet-propulsion backpack gave him the edge over his enemies. It could launch an explosive and destructive rocket. He travelled aboard his starship, *Slave I.*

DARTH TYRANUS

About a decade before to the outbreak of the Clone Wars, a man named Tyranus approached Jango and made a surprising proposal. He wanted Jango to become the template of a clone army in exchange for a large fee.

Fett agreed on one condition. In addition to his fee, he wanted an unaltered clone of himself. This clone would not undergo the growth acceleration or docility tampering to which the others would be exposed. It would be a pure replica of Jango.

FATHER AND SON

Fett had his own apartment in the Kaminoan Tipoca City, and cut down his work as a bounty hunter. Instead, he focused on teaching his 'son', Boba, about survival and combat while the Kaminoans continued the process of building thousands of clone soldiers. Fett wanted to see what his life might have been like had he been raised by a caring guardian. Still, if the credits were right or the challenge appealed to him, he would don his battle armour periodically and venture from his hiding place.

Jango Fett was a deadly marksman and a master of unarmed combat.

TENACIOUS OBI-WAN KENOBI

Jedi Master Obi-Wan Kenobi was not prepared to forget about the attempt on Senator Amidala or the death of Zam Wesell. Jango had used a Kamino saberdart to eliminate Zam. Although all mention of Kamino had been wiped from the Jedi Archives, Obi-Wan's underworld contacts were able to point him in the right direction.

Kenobi arrived on Kamino and learned of the clone army. When he confronted Jango, the bounty hunter realised that it was time for him to leave the planet. He told Boba to gather their belongings. As they were about to leave, the Jedi Master tried to stop them and Jango fought him on the rain-swept landing platforms of Tipoca City.

Jango escaped aboard the *Slave I*, heading for Geonosis and Lord Tyranus. However, Obi-Wan had placed a homing beacon on their vessel and he pursued them in his starfighter.

ASSASSIN FOR HIRE

Viceroy Nute Gunray of the Trade Federation hired Jango to assassinate Senator Padmé Amidala, against whom he had harboured a deep grudge since she humiliated him during the siege of Naboo. Fett subcontracted the job to the bounty hunter Zam Wesell, and armed her with poisonous kouhuns. However, a pair of meddling Jedi got in the way of the hit, and Jango was forced to kill Zam to prevent the trail from leading back to him.

DEATH ON GEONOSIS

It was on Geonosis that Jango finally met his end. Although Obi-Wan was captured by the Geonosians, Jedi Knights arrived just in time. They brought with them part of the clone army that the Kaminoans had created.

Jango entered the fight against the Jedi and his blaster skills killed several of them. However, he was no match for Mace Windu. The Jedi Master swiftly cut off the bounty hunter's head with a single stroke of his lightsaber. Jango's battle-dented helmet was picked up by Boba Fett. Echoing his clone parent's life, he too was now an orphan and would have to fend for himself.

BOBA FETT

Boba watched helplessly as Mace Windu beheaded his father, Jango Fett, at the start of the Battle of Geonosis.

IDENTITY FILE

Boba Fett was the 'son' of Jango Fett and a merciless bounty hunter, famous and dreaded throughout the galaxy. His ship was knows as *Slave I* and his usual weapon was the BlasTech EE-3 rifle. In actual fact, Boba Fett was not Jango's son, but his clone, an exact genetic replica of his 'father'. Boba hero-worshipped his father and became a bounty hunter to follow in his footsteps.

EARLY YEARS

As part of Jango's payment for being the genetic host of the clone army, he was given a clone that was not modified in any way. He named the clone Boba and raised him as a son. From Jango, Boba learned valuable survival and martial skills, and even as a child he was proficient with a blaster and laser cannon.

Fett was raised in isolation on Kamino, but his life was turned upside down when Obi-Wan Kenobi came looking for his father. Kenobi brawled with Jango as the Fetts tried to escape from Kamino. Boba helped his father by pinning the Jedi down with explosive laser fire from the Fett starship, *Slave I.*

The Fetts retreated to Geonosis. Obi-Wan pursued them, but he was captured and sentenced to death. However, a huge battle erupted as Jedi reinforcements stormed Geonosis to free their fellow Jedi. Jango entered the fray, only to be killed by Jedi Master Mace Windu.

Boba was shocked and horrified by his father's swift death, and he quietly cradled Jango's empty helmet as Geonosis erupted into all-out war.

FRIGHTENING ARMOUR

After Geonosis, Boba Fett donned the Mandalorian armour of his fallen father. The Mandalorians were a nomadic warrior sect founded over 4,000 years before the Galactic Civil War. Jango Fett served as leader of the Mandalorians until they were wiped out at Galidraan decades before the Clone Wars. Jango retained the Mandalorian armour applying his years of experience to his new role as the galaxy's greatest bounty hunter - a mantle that would be passed on to Boba.

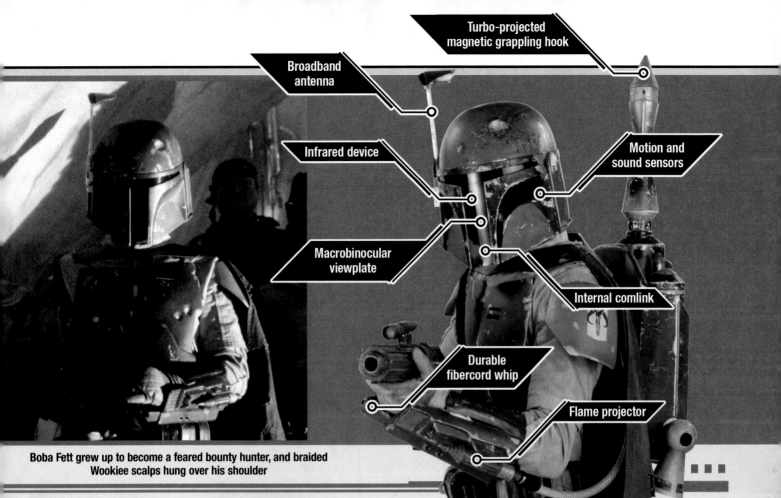

Broadband antenna

Turbo-projected magnetic grappling hook

Infrared device

Motion and sound sensors

Macrobinocular viewplate

Internal comlink

Durable fibercord whip

Flame projector

Knee-pad rocket dart launchers

Spiked boots

Boba Fett grew up to become a feared bounty hunter, and braided Wookiee scalps hung over his shoulder

HAN SOLO

Fett earned his largest fortune with the capture of Han Solo on Cloud City because both Darth Vader and Jabba the Hutt paid a reward for him. He also angered several other bounty hunters, including Bossk and IG-88. They jealously followed him until he safely delivered Solo's body, which was frozen in carbonite, to Jabba.

When Luke, Leia and Chewbacca were captured while trying to rescue Han, Boba Fett was still with the Hutt lord. Jabba sentenced them to a slow death by sarlacc, but the Rebels put up an almighty fight. During the tussle, Han Solo accidentally knocked Fett into the sarlacc's gullet. It seemed as though Boba Fett was doomed to remain there, suffering unimaginable torture for 1000 years as the sarlacc slowly digested him. However, Fett was the only known person ever to escape the pit of the sarlacc. He reappeared and continued to pursue Han Solo with renewed venom.

TAKING A GAMBLE

After delivering Han Solo to Jabba the Hutt, Boba Fett remained at the crime lord's side. The Hutt proposed some underground demolition events and Fett gladly entered. From the very first match, he became Jabba's reigning champion and his matches became major gambling events.

THE CLONE WARS

IDENTITY FILE

The Clone Wars were a time of violence and unrest throughout the galaxy. The Separatists wanted to change the very nature of the corrupt and bureaucratic Republic. Led by Count Dooku and secretly supported by the mysterious Darth Sidious, the Separatists spread dissent, swelling their ranks with those who lusted after power and riches, including the money-hungry Confederacy of Independent Systems.

The Battle of Geonosis was the first engagement of the wars, and it was a terrifying and saddening day. Seemingly endless legions of clone troopers were led into battle by Jedi Knights, and it marked the beginning of a conflict that would last for years, spreading a dark stain of violence across the galaxy where the Jedi had once worked so hard to maintain peace.

After the clone army was discovered by Obi-Wan Kenobi, they were put into the service of the Republic. The massive military force deeply worried the members of the Jedi Order.

PALPATINE

Chancellor Palpatine was the puppet master who engineered the Clone Wars in order to destroy the Republic and rule the galaxy himself. In his disguise as Darth Sidious, the evil Sith Master, he arranged for a clone army to be built and incited the Separatists to commit acts of invasion, assassination and kidnapping. As Palpatine, he advocated a military response to the increasing separatist threat.

The Clone Wars raged for years as he pulled the strings. Thousands died in the conflicts and the Republic grew increasingly more vulnerable.

For years Palpatine cultivated the trust and friendship of Jedi Anakin Skywalker. He realised that Skywalker was strong in the Force, and he was determined to turn him to the dark side.

At last the moment Palpatine had been working towards arrived. The Jedi were scattered across the galaxy and the massive clone army was under his absolute command. Palpatine revealed his true Sith nature to Skywalker and succeeded in turning the young man to the dark side. Naming Skywalker Darth Vader, he sent him to slaughter the innocent Jedi younglings in the Temple. He also issued Order 66 to every commander in his clone army.

Across the galaxy, the clone soldiers turned on their Jedi leaders and massacred them. With the Jedi destroyed, Palpatine knew that there was no one to stand in his way. He became Emperor and set about washing away the last remnants of the once-splendid Republic.

CLONE COMMANDER CODY (UNIT 2224)

Clone Commander Cody was a loyal clone trooper and a member of the clone army that served the Galactic Republic during the Clone Wars. Cody was often under the command of General Obi-Wan Kenobi, and served alongside him and Anakin Skywalker during a dangerous campaign on Cato Neimoidia.

Cody had a close and friendly relationship with Kenobi and shared his dry sense of humour. This camaraderie was a great help during their mission to Utapau, where they went to search for the Separatist forces commanded by General Grievous.

However, Cody was a servant of the Republic and his clone upbringing had made him obedient above all else. When Order 66 branded Kenobi an enemy of the state, Cody willingly carried out the command to open fire on his former friend.

CLONE TROOPERS

DID YOU KNOW?

A finned SCUBA trooper version also existed.

Sometimes clone troopers wore ponchos in inclement weather and terrain.

The Kaminoan cloners reconditioned an average of seven aberrants for every 200 clones produced, maintaining superb standards.

The Kaminoans used methods of absolute sterilisation and super-clean surfaces. Such standards were extraordinary for so vast an enterprise, and Obi-Wan Kenobi was astonished when he first discovered this vast army in waiting.

IDENTITY FILE

Clone troopers were identical in physical appearance, mental capability and stamina, and they were impossible to tell apart. They were grown in the cloning facilities of the Kaminoan Tipoca City, as part of a clone army. They were all based on exactly the same genetic host, Jango Fett, but their genetic mental structure was altered to make them less independent, and their growth was accelerated to twice the normal rate of a human. They were grown and trained specifically for military combat.

THE LIFE OF A CLONE

The stress of accelerated growth, physically, mentally or emotionally, could have driven a clone insane. To prevent this, the Kaminoans made sure that the future army was developed within a highly disciplined and balanced programme. Batches of clones were trained with exactly enough semblance of community to make them emotionally stable. Physical skills were imparted through learning devices and perfected through practice. At a physical age of just ten years, the clones were fully developed and ready for battle, although they did not have normal personalities.

JANGO FETT

Once fully grown, all clones looked exactly like their genetic host. Jango Fett lived on Kamino and helped to train the troopers, knowing better than anyone how best to guide their development and teach them military skills.

THE FIRST BATTLE OF THE CLONE WARS

On Geonosis, the Republic deployed two full battle armies, with Yoda and Mace Windu commanding one each. Other veteran Jedi Knights were in charge of eight corps of 36,864 troops each. Specially trained clones led all other divisions. Commanders headed regiments of 2,304 men; clone captains led companies of 144 men; lieutenants headed platoons of 36 men and sergeants commanded squads, each made up of nine clone troopers. Separate ranks of specialised clones operated gunships, drop ships, AT-TEs and SPHA-Ts. In total, 192,000 clone troopers were deployed that day.

The first combat in which the clone troopers were used was the Battle of Geonosis, which marked the beginning of the Clone Wars.

THE LARS FAMILY

CLIEGG LARS

Cliegg Lars was modest and good-hearted. During a trip to the bustling spaceport of Mos Eisley, he met and fell in love with Shmi Skywalker, who was a slave owned by Watto the junk trader.

Cliegg bought Shmi and married her, bringing her home to his moisture farm. They lived happily together for years, creating a warm and friendly home for themselves and Cliegg's son, Owen. However, the Lars family was not destined for peace and tranquility. Early one morning while she was picking mushrooms, Shmi was attacked and abducted by the savage Tusken Raiders.

Cliegg led a posse of friends out into the desert to find her. It was a massacre. Of the 30 farmers he took, only four returned alive. Cliegg lost his leg and could not continue the search because of his wounds. He believed that Shmi was dead. Because he could no longer walk, he used a hovering mechno-chair.

A month after Cliegg had given Shmi up for dead, Anakin Skywalker arrived at the farm. When he heard what had happened he raced off into the desert to find his mother. Many hours later he returned with her body. In a quiet funeral, Shmi was buried at the Lars homestead. Cliegg said that she had been the most loving partner that any man could ever have.

OWEN LARS

Owen Lars valued the discipline and work ethic that his father had taught him. Even as a young man, he always knew that he wanted to remain on Tatooine. His goal was to make the moisture farm successful and productive, and to live there with his true love, Beru.

This simple ambition was complicated by the arrival of his baby nephew, Luke Skywalker. He and Beru were made the boy's wards, but Owen harboured resentful feelings towards his stepbrother, Anakin, and Obi-Wan Kenobi. This resentment would affect many of the things he chose to teach Luke.

Owen tried to bring up his nephew as a normal boy, concealing all knowledge of his Jedi heritage. He told Luke that his father was dead and that he had been a freighter navigator. He cared deeply about Luke, but he could be gruff and strict, which often led to tension between him and his daydreaming nephew.

However, he could not control Luke's thirst for adventure. Young Skywalker dreamed of leaving Tatooine and joining the Imperial Academy, where he would learn to fly among the stars. Year after year, Lars refused to allow him to go, fearing that he would fall victim to his father's fate.

BERU LARS

Beru's aspirations never reached beyond marrying the man she loved and living with him on Tatooine. The life of a moisture farmer was tough, but she took it on willingly. Along with her husband, she worked season after season, under harsh conditions, to extract precious water from the environment.

Beru was a substitute mother to Luke Skywalker and she thought that he should be allowed to go to the Academy. Like her husband, Beru became another victim of the cruel Empire when stormtroopers raided the farm.

TUSKEN RAIDERS

There was a deeply rooted gender divide within Tusken society. The females tended to the camps while the males ventured out to hunt and fight. Tusken children wore their unisex garments in order to make it impossible to visually determine their gender.

IDENTITY FILE

Tusken Raiders were nomadic and violent desert savages who lived among the rocky Jundland Wastes of Tatooine. Because of them, colonists rarely wandered far from their communities. The Tusken Raiders, or Sand People as they were also known, were extremely territorial and xenophobic. They were prepared to attack with almost no provocation. They travelled in single file to conceal their numbers.

CLOTHING

Tusken Raiders dressed in tattered rags from head to foot, and they carried gaderffii, which were clubs with blades on them. They also carried projectile rifles with which to shoot at passing vehicles.

The male of the species tended to be the most aggressive. Females wore elaborate jewelled masks with eye-slits and long shrouds that covered their whole body. Tusken children wore unisex cowls and simple cloaks.

TRANSPORT

The Sand People needed transportation and so they domesticated the bantha, which was a beast also found on Tatooine. Strangely, the Tuskens had developed an almost telepathic link with the bantha and the beasts were very important in their culture. They were intrinsically connected, almost as if they made each other whole. A tribe member who had lost his bantha was considered incomplete and an outcast. When a raider died, his mount would become frenzied and suicidal. Such crazed banthas were set loose in the desert.

The nomadic Tuskens travelled in family groups of 20 to 30 with their banthas. The desert could be a cruel and deadly place, and Tuskens were taught the secrets of desert survival as early in their lives as possible. They had to complete a ritual rite of passage before being accepted as adults. Such trials could include hunting and slaying a krayt dragon or raiding an outlander camp.

The Tusken Raiders traveled on banthas, which were long haired and spiral-horned.

SACRED LAND

When the colonists arrived on Tatooine, they set up a number of communities before encountering the Sand People. One such outpost was Fort Tusken, northwest of Mos Eisley. The settlers built their fort on land that was sacred to the nomadic people. They carried out a brutal and bloody attack on the colonist community. The name 'Tusken Raider' was born from that day, as was the permanent state of tension between the Sand People and the outlanders.

SOCIETY

Although very little was known about the Sand People, it was believed that they were the descendents of the Ghorfas, a society that built caves within cliffs. Their civilization collapsed when the colonists disrupted their water supply, and this led to the development of their nomadic existence.

Once each year, all new adults were paired for life in a ceremony that involved the mixing of the blood of husband and wife, and their respective bantha mounts. Then, in the privacy of a tent, the couple would unwrap their bindings and show each other their true forms. Only their mate was allowed to know their true appearance. Even an accidental glimpse of an unwrapped Tusken resulted in a blood duel.

STORYTELLING

Tuskens lived a life of strict ritual and immoveable rules. They had a rich oral history which was always retold by a respected Raider known as the storyteller. At each telling, the storyteller had to repeat the detailed Tusken stories of the past word for word. It was blasphemy to get a single word wrong, and if a storyteller made a mistake the punishment was instant death.

When Tusken Raiders tortured and killed his mother, Anakin Skywalker ignored his Jedi training and slaughtered the Sand People in a bloodthirsty rage. Neither man, woman nor child escaped his bright blade.

GEONOSIANS

Despite their thin build, Geonosians were extremely strong. Their tough exoskeletons gave them protection from physical damage and from the bouts of radiation that showered Geonosis.

IDENTITY FILE

There were two main types of Geonosian: the wingless worker drones and the winged aristocrats. Certain features were common to all types, including their hard exoskeletons, elongated faces, multi-jointed limbs and clicking language.

GEONOSIS

Geonosis was a forbidding, rocky world less than a parsec away from Tatooine. It was a ringed planet with barren deserts and craggy, red rocks. The inhabitants of Geonosis evolved to survive in the harsh ecology. The planet's remote location and its droid foundries made it an ideal headquarters for the Separatist movement.

GEONOSIAN ENTERTAINMENT

Geonosians had an extremely barbaric side to their nature. They saw brutal violence as entertainment, and anyone condemned to die was forced to do so in front of a cheering audience. The Geonosians congregated in massive execution arenas to watch victims being fed to savage creatures. They liked to see the victims put up a bit of a fight, but this culture of blood-lust got more than it bargained for when it tried to execute Obi-Wan, Anakin and Padmé. Instead of having the thrill of watching the spies ripped apart, the Geonosians cowered in terror as the first battle of the Clone Wars swung into action.

The inhabitants of Geonosis were insectoids whose society was divided by a strict caste system. They lived in hive colonies within gigantic, organic-looking spires.

CASTE SYSTEM

Geonosians were born into specific castes divided along the lines of their physical attributes.

Though most Geonosians were happy to spend all their lives within their assigned caste, a few developed ambition and aspired to ascend socially.

The aristocrats were cruel to the workers, forcing them to work no matter the conditions or the danger. These ruling members thought they had the right to force thousands of workers to labour for their whims.

A lower-caste Geonosian had one chance to escape their bonds – gladiatorial combat. For the pleasure and entertainment of the aristocrats, members of the lower castes were pitted against each other or against savage creatures in their immense arenas. A Geonosian who repeatedly won and survived such 'games' could achieve celebrity status and ascend socially. Others would work towards the day when they had earned enough wealth to leave the planet altogether.

APPEARANCE

The winged Geonosian soldier drones became adults very quickly and were ready for combat at the age of six. They were intelligent enough to protect the hive from natural predators, but they could be easily outwitted and conquered by those with more intelligence.

There was a separate caste for those Geonosians who were raised to be pilots. They were extremely tough and they did not need any sleep. In training, each pilot pupa would pair forever with a fighter's flight computer. They then developed a rapport that gave them an extra edge in their role.

HIVE SWEET HIVE

The inhabitants of the planet rarely left Geonosis. The importance of the hive was ingrained from birth, and they looked down on other species. The few Geonosians that did venture offworld usually did so as work groups that ultimately benefited their home hives. Geonosian contractors could be found at Baktoid Combat Automata plants across the Rim.

BAIL ORGANA

Senator Bail Organa of Alderaan was a trusted advisor in Chancellor Palpatine's inner circle. He was deeply saddened when, to counter the Separatist threat, the Republic had to deploy their newly-discovered clone army.

As the Senate grew more and more corrupt, Bail Organa began to see that Chancellor Palpatine had become a virtual dictator. After the true horror of Palpatine's plan was unveiled, Organa became a friend of the Rebel Alliance, working to overthrow the Empire.

A TROUBLED START

Though he grew to become a beloved leader on Alderaan, Bail Organa's ascent to that position was not without controversy. For a brief time before Organa inherited the Viceroy title, there was a dispute regarding the appropriate lineage of ascendancy. After three deadlocked votes, a special dispatch from the Republic government in the form of Jedi Jorus C'baoth was sent to oversee the ascendancy. C'baoth guided the tribunal to the decision that saw the appointment of Organa.

A KIND SENATOR

Organa was a compassionate man and championed benevolent causes such as the Refugee Relief Movement. With his approval, Alderaan loosened its immigration restrictions to allow an influx of refugees displaced by the growing Separatist crisis that preceded the Clone Wars. He was critical of policies that targeted the downtrodden, such as a Senate-approved transit tax that made it difficult for refugees to resettle.

After enduring a number of miscarriages, Bail Organa's wife was delighted to adopt the baby Leia.

HIDDEN DANGERS

Bail began to question the war effort when he learned that much of the information regarding the war was being withheld from the Senate. He became even more convinced when he saw the destruction of a freighter that killed Finis Valorum. From then on, he was consistently opposing the growing war powers that were granted to Palpatine.

THE YEARS OF THE EMPIRE

Bail Organa and Senator Mon Mothma thought it was likely that Palpatine would not want to give up power once the Clone Wars ended. They secretly put plans into motion to create an organisation that was dedicated to preserving the ideals of the Republic.

After the issue of Order 66, Organa tried to get to the bottom of the assault on the Jedi Temple. Instead, he was turned away by the clone troopers, who told him a Jedi rebellion was afoot. Bail saw them shoot a young Padawan and realised that all the Jedi were at risk. Risking everything, Organa rescued Yoda and Obi-Wan. However, he then received an urgent call from Coruscant — the Chancellor was calling an emergency session of congress. He returned to the capital with Obi-Wan and Yoda aboard. Bail arrived at the Senate just in time to hear Chancellor Palpatine declare himself Emperor. His worst fears had come to pass. The Republic was dead, the Jedi Order was in tatters and a merciless dictatorship had taken command of the galaxy.

A HOPE FOR THE FUTURE

In the hope that one day the new Empire would be defeated, Bail agreed to raise the orphaned child Leia, the daughter of Padmé and the fallen Jedi Anakin Skywalker. He and his wife brought her up and loved her as if she had been their own daughter.

Leia followed in her adopted father's footsteps and became the youngest member of the Imperial Senate. Secretly, she also supported the Rebel Alliance, using her diplomatic immunity to smuggle supplies and information to Rebels.

Together, the Organas gathered technical information about the Empire's secret weapon, the dreaded Death Star, in the hope that they would discover how to destroy it. Bail sent Leia on a mission to find Obi-Wan Kenobi and recruit him into the Alliance to help face the Death Star challenge. While Leia was still struggling to fulfill this mission, Bail was killed when the Death Star destroyed Alderaan.

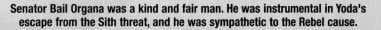

Senator Bail Organa was a kind and fair man. He was instrumental in Yoda's escape from the Sith threat, and he was sympathetic to the Rebel cause.

CHEWBACCA AND THE WOOKIEES

Years before he befriended smuggler Han Solo and became the first mate and copilot of the *Millennium Falcon*, the Wookiee warrior Chewbacca served under the command of Jedi Master Yoda in the Clone Wars.

IDENTITY FILE

Born on the tree-filled planet of Kashyyyk, the 200-year-old Chewbacca saw life as a slave, a smuggler, and a top-notch pilot and mechanic.

He was a loyal and brave friend, but a frightening enemy. He could tear the limbs off of most creatures barehanded and his weapon of choice was a bowcaster, a handcrafted crossbow-like weapon that shot explosive packets of energy. A bandolier slung from Chewbacca's left shoulder contained enough extra firepower to take on a squad of stormtroopers. But sometimes his terrifying growls and roars - the basis of the Wookiee language - masked his fear.

YODA'S LIFE

Loyal even at great personal risk, strong as a gladiator, and as savvy as the brightest Academy graduate, Chewbacca was a true hero of the Clone Wars. With his fellow warrior Tarfful, he was always prepared for battle. When Palpatine gave Order 66 and the clone troopers turned on the Jedi, Chewbacca was with General Yoda. He and Tarfful displayed the ferocity and courage that Wookiees are known for when they helped Yoda escape the attack.

HARD LABOUR

Many years later, when he was being mistreated at a hard-labour camp, Chewbacca was saved from certain death by a young Han Solo. As a result, Chewbacca swore a 'life debt' to Solo and became first the protector and then the best friend of the Corellian. He served with Solo as he embarked on a smuggling career, aided by the swift *Millennium Falcon*.

Chewbacca went on to become one of the heroes of the Rebel Alliance and the New Republic.

SMUGGLERS

On one spice-smuggling run, for which they had been hired by crime lord Jabba the Hutt, Solo and Chewbacca had to dump their cargo before being boarded by Imperials. They had to face Jabba back on Tatooine. But before visiting the Hutt's palace, they met the Obi-Wan Kenobi in the Mos Eisley cantina. He had a job for them that promised a payment big enough to calm Jabba. Little did they know that this moment would change their lives. Within a short time, the partners had helped rescue a princess, blown up the Empire's top-secret battle station and been declared heroes by the Rebel Alliance.

GENERAL GRIEVOUS

When the greedy corporations and systems of the galaxy pooled their resources, they became the Confederacy of Independent Systems. Their military assets formed a droid army of seemingly limitless size. But they needed a mastermind to control that army effectively.

From within the ranks of the Confederacy came General Grievous, a brilliant strategist without compassion. His unorthodox fighting form and mechanical enhancements gave him an edge in close-quarters battle. He was trained in lightsaber combat by Darth Tyranus, and his ingenuity and cunning made him almost invincible against the Jedi. He became Supreme Commander of the droid armies.

INDESTRUCTIBLE

Grievous was an alien who was connected with the Banking Clan. Long before the Clone Wars, he was already a great military leader, fighter and strategist. But then he had a horrible accident that nearly took his life. So he allowed the Geonosians to construct a durasteel shell for what little of him remained. It took him a long time to come to terms with his new self. Then he was presented to Count Dooku, and his real training began. In mere weeks he had surpassed any of Dooku's previous students. It helped, of course, to have an indestructible body.

Grievous hunted Jedi for sport. Part non-humanoid alien, part custom-designed droid, he displayed his victims' lightsabers around his belt as trophies of his victories.

A BRAVE WARRIOR

Though Grievous orchestrated many campaigns from sheltered bunkers, he was not afraid to fight alongside his soulless troops in the frontlines of the battlegrounds. Jedi General Daakman Barrek first reported Grievous' frightening form on the industrial world of Hypori, where Grievous laid waste to almost all of Barrek's forces.

PALPATINE'S PLAN

Grievous thought that he had struck his greatest blow when he invaded the capital and abducted Chancellor Palpatine, the leader of the Galactic Senate. He was not aware that Sidious and Palpatine were one and the same.

Palpatine knew that Grievous and his whole army didn't stand a chance against Anakin Skywalker. What he wanted to know was whether or not Anakin could stand up against a Sith Lord - could he beat Dooku? Palpatine's real intention, if Anakin was good enough, was to allow him to kill Dooku and then become a Sith apprentice. However, he didn't tell Dooku that...

JEDI JUSTICE

After Dooku's death, Grievous fled to Utapau. He was pursued by Obi-Wan Kenobi, with whom he engaged in hand-to-hand combat. Noticing that the general's stomach plate was loose, Obi-Wan ripped it off and saw a bag that contained Grievous' organic innards. Obi-Wan fired a blaster into Grievous's stomach and the general exploded from the inside out.

With his hardened alloy body, six fingers on each hand, gold-coloured eyes with reptilian pupils and blood-red sockets, Grievous was a frightening spectacle. After a long battle, Obi-Wan was able to defeat him.

DROIDS

Battle droids were the foot soldiers of the Trade Federation army.

DROIDS

During the last decades of the Republic, the Jedi Order had replaced any need for a unified military for protection. Instead, private interests maintained their own armed forces. The commercial organisations could afford the most powerful and most effective armies.

Despite legislation to curb the potency of any one private army, the massive corporations were able to build massive droid forces. Though no one droid army would pose a threat to the Republic, the Separatist movement pooled these resources into a terrifying military power.

IDENTITY FILE

Under the control of the Neimoidians, the battle droids served as security, ground troops and pilots of the Trade Federation battleships. Their strength was in their great numbers and eerily automated discipline. Battle droids worked by attacking in massive waves and overwhelming their enemies.

Droids were not programmed for independent thought, and their intelligence was derived from a central source aboard the Trade Federation droid control ship. They were mindless, but unquestioningly obedient. The battle droid was a staple of the Trade Federation army.

SPECIALISED TYPES OF DROID WERE DISTINGUISHED BY COLOUR:
Yellow = commanders
Blue = pilots
Maroon = security guards

Battle droids were tall, gaunt humanoids with exposed joints and bone-white metal finishes that made them look like skeletons.

SECRET ARMIES

Battle droids were produced in massive foundries on the rocky planet Geonosis. After the Trade Federation used battle droids to hold Naboo captive, they were given a court order to reduce the battle droid armies. However, Geonosian foundries continued to run at maximum capacity. Under the supervision of Archduke of Geonosis Poggle the Lesser, thousands more battle droids joined the ranks of the Trade Federation armies, secretly massing on Geonosis.

MINDLESS WEAPONS

The cost of thousands of individual droid brains was avoided by relying on a Central Control Computer (CCC). The command and security-division droids had some level of autonomy, but all battle droids were obedient to the commands of the CCC. If a droid lost contact with the control signal, it entered a standby hibernating mode.

DID YOU KNOW?

All battle droids had a number printed on their back.

Regular infantry battle droids carried backpacks at all times. Commander droids had smaller, back-mounted communication units. Security and pilot battle droids had no backpacks.

Battle droids were 6'3".

Modified versions included flame, plasma, and rifle battle droids. Other versions were the bomb droid, grenade droids, and gunner droids.

Commander battle droids could speak and were often the droids on Trade Federation tanks/AATs.

If damaged, a battle droid deactivated the electromagnets holding its joints together. Though this made the droid fragile, it prevented the spread of damage and allowed the droids to be salvaged for future repair and reuse.

HAILFIRE DROID

The hailfire droid was a self-aware mobile missile-platform used exclusively by the IG Banking Clan. It delivered surface-to-surface and surface-to-air strikes with stacked banks of 30 rocket warheads. Hailfires rolled along on oversized hoop-like wheels. A small, central body was equipped with a single photoreceptor. When the InterGalactic Banking Clan pledged its forces to the Confederacy of Independent Systems, its hailfire droids were added to the immense Separatist droid army.

HOMING SPIDER DROID

The homing spider droid was a large, mobile engine of destruction used in the Commerce Guild's private droid army. It was designed for anti-vehicular combat. The orb-shaped central body was equipped with sensor equipment and a powerful laser cannon that could fire a sustained beam at enemy targets. It moved on all-terrain stilt-like legs.

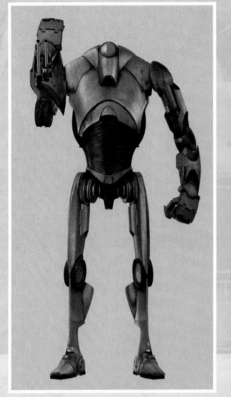

SUPER BATTLE DROID

The super battle droid required no overriding command signal in order to operate, and therefore had a limited degree of independence. Its delicate inner workings were protected by a hardened armoured body-case. Mounted on its right manipulator was a double-laser cannon built into the droid's design.

Super battle droids, like their predecessors, had very basic programming and were poor at formulating attack plans. They were, however, fearless and tireless, and would run at full speed into combat, their cannons extended, firing until they had reduced their targets to smouldering ruins.

DWARF SPIDER DROID

The Commerce Guild brought their dwarf spider droids into the Separatist ranks. The four-legged, dome-shaped mechanical arachnid featured a powerful, centrally mounted laser cannon.

DARTH VADER

IDENTITY FILE

Darth Vader was a Dark Lord of the Sith, apprentice to Emperor Palpatine, and one of the most feared of Palpatine's aides. He terrorized the galaxy hunting the last of the Jedi Order and eliminating all who stood in his path without mercy. Vader used a masterful knowledge of the dark side of the Force to torture and kill all his enemies - and even his allies if they displeased him.

A final confrontation with his old Master, Obi-Wan Kenobi, left Darth Vader mortally wounded on the fiery planet of Mustafar. The Emperor rescued him and took him to an Imperial rehabilitation centre. It was here that Vader's gnarled and amputated body was fused to cyborg limbs and encased in his fearsome black suit. He was kept alive by an artificial respiration unit inside his suit and an unbending and vengeful evil that he channelled from the dark side of the Force.

After learning the identity of the Rebel pilot who destroyed the Death Star, Vader scoured the galaxy for Luke Skywalker. During their confrontation on Bespin, Vader revealed a terrible secret.

TIME FILE

-19	Becomes Darth Vader
-19	Defeated by Obi-Wan during a duel on Mustafar
-19	Palpatine brings Vader to Coruscant where he is fitted with life-supporting black armour.
-19	Luke and Leia born
0	Captures Princess Leia following the theft of the plans to the Death Star
0	Battle of Yavin
1	Learns that Luke Skywalker destroyed the Death Star
3	Duels Luke Skywalker at Bespin
4	Duels Luke Skywalker aboard the second Death Star
4	Turns against the Emperor to save Luke
4	Becomes one with the Force

THE MASSACRE OF THE INNOCENTS

As Anakin accepted the dark side of the Force, Palpatine bestowed upon him the name of Darth Vader and he became Palpatine's new apprentice and a Dark Lord of the Sith. Although a battle still raged inside him, Anakin could think only of saving Amidala and that meant swearing loyalty to Palpatine. Together, Palpatine convinced him, they would use the dark side to ensure she lived through childbirth.

In Sith Lore it is demanded that the apprentice shows undivided loyalty to the Sith. Palpatine gave Vader a terrible mission. He convinced Vader that all Jedi were the enemies of the Republic and that as long as a single one remained alive there would never be peace in the galaxy. The first task was to lead the attack on the Jedi Temple where the future of the Jedi Order trained.

Anakin Skywalker was a hero to the young Jedi at the Temple, but when he entered with the clone troopers of the 501st Legion, all his heroism had been cast aside. He had allowed himself to be consumed with the dark side of the Force and led a massacre that left smoke rising from the towers of the Temple. His anger had made him strong and the more he gave way to it, the stronger he became.

"YOU HAVE BECOME THE VERY THING YOU SWORE TO DESTROY."

THE ULTIMATE ENFORCER

Darth Vader served the Emperor closely and he made it his mission to seek out and destroy any of the Jedi survivors of Order 66. There were only a handful of Jedi remaining but, through various torture methods, Vader discovered their whereabouts and hunted them down to near extinction.

Vader was also head of an operation to search and destroy all elements of a Rebel Alliance that had grown into a formidable enemy. The Rebels even got hold of the plans to the Emperor's Death Star and Palpatine instructed Vader to find them as a matter of urgency.

Darth Vader tracked the Death Star plans to a ship belonging to Princess Leia Organa, a senator from the planet Alderaan. He captured her ship and tortured her to discover the whereabouts of the plans and the Rebel headquarters. Vader and Grand Moff Tarkin took Leia back to Alderaan aboard the Death Star and made her watch the destruction of her home planet.

After Darth Vader returned from Bespin the Emperor assigned him to oversee the construction of a new Death Star. Vader and the Emperor plotted to lure Skywalker aboard and turn him to the dark side of the Force.

FATHER AND SON

At the Battle of Yavin, Vader took to the skies in his modified TIE fighter to deal with the threat of the Rebel X-wing fighters. He almost prevented the destruction of the Death Star single-handedly, but was eluded by a pilot in whom the Force was unnervingly strong. The young Rebel pilot named Luke Skywalker stirred some strange feelings from the dark recesses of Vader's past.

Vader tirelessly tracked the Rebels to discover their new base, but he held a secret desire to find Luke above all else. A conflict of interest had risen between his loyalty to the Emperor and the feelings he felt on discovering that his son was alive. On the Emperor's instruction, Vader was to find Luke and kill him, but Vader suggested that they lure Luke to the dark side of the Force. The Emperor agreed but was suspicious of Vader's motives.

Using Luke's friends as bait, Vader lured Luke into a trap and cut off his hand in a lightsaber duel. He revealed that he was Luke's father and suggested they join forces and destroy the Emperor. Luke would not turn to the dark side and escaped his father.

The next time they met, Luke was much more powerful and the Emperor engineered a stage for Luke to destroy Vader and become Palpatine's new Sith apprentice. Luke almost succumbed but once again denied the dark side of the Force. Palpatine turned on him with Force lightning and Vader felt within a terrible conflict within himself.

Vader picked up the Emperor and threw him down into the reactor core of the Death Star, mortally wounding himself in the process. Vader had turned from the dark side of the Force and before he died, Luke removed Vader's mask to see the eyes of his father, Anakin Skywalker. His body became one with the Force and Luke cremated the suit that had for so long symbolised evil throughout the galaxy.

Darth Vader was one of the Emperor's most loyal servants and the most ruthless enforcer of his will. He mercilessly dealt with Rebel spies and opponents of the Galactic Empire.

THE EMPIRE

The Emperor inspired terror and horror in equal measures, ruling the galaxy with cruel command and reveling in his own power. Having destroyed the Jedi Order and the Republic, and having turned the Chosen One to the dark side, he could not believe that the Rebel Alliance had a chance of stopping him.

IDENTITY FILE

Many hoped that the Galactic Empire would sweep away the injustices and corruption of its predecessor, the Galactic Republic. However, the Empire became a tyrannical regime. After his fight with Mace Windu, Palpatine was horribly disfigured. He withdrew more and more, becoming a terrifying and mysterious shadow figure. His true despotic nature was revealed, and he instilled fear into all his subjects. Personal liberties were crushed, and the governance of everyday affairs was removed from the Senate and given to corrupt regional governors.

As the Empire grew, so did its military. Shipyards churned out vast fleets of Star Destroyers and TIE fighters. Without the Jedi to maintain order in the galaxy, the job was given to the Imperial Starfleet.

REBELLION

The people over whom the Empire ruled were not without spirit, and a rebellious streak could be found in most places throughout the galaxy. However, the Emperor taught his officers that the most effective method of ruling was fear. The power hungry lieutenants and technocrats developed increasingly powerful instruments of destruction to cow a rebellious populace.

Despite this tyranny, rebellious feelings could not be crushed. Small pockets of resistance banded together to form the Alliance to Restore the Republic.

THE EMPEROR'S LAST PLOT

The Battle of Endor was entirely engineered by the prescient Emperor Palpatine, just as he had once engineered the start of the Clone Wars. He intended the Battle of Endor to be the final confrontation in the Galactic Civil War. However, he failed to foresee the resourcefulness of the Rebels or the treachery of one of his most trusted aides.

Although he had seemed almost indestructible, Palpatine died at Endor. The second Death Star was destroyed by the valiant pilots of the Rebel Alliance. With these crippling blows, the Imperial reign of terror over the galaxy ended. The Rebellion began forming a New Republic, and across the galaxy the worlds celebrated their newfound freedom.

THE DEATH STAR

The Death Star was the ultimate instrument of destruction - the weapon of weapons. It was a mobile space station with a prime weapon of unspeakable power. When fully charged, the Death Star's superlaser had the ability to destroy a planet.

To the Emperor's fury, the Rebel Alliance destroyed the Death Star at the Battle of Yavin. Determined to crush the Rebels once and for all, the Emperor charged Darth Vader with finding and destroying the Rebels. After three years of searching he finally located their headquarters and routed them at the Battle of Hoth.

A few months later, the Rebels made a sickening discovery. The Death Star had not been the only Imperial superweapon in development. A second Death Star was nearing completion over the distant moon of Endor, and Palpatine himself would be present for the final stages of construction. The temptation was immense; the Empire's incomplete great weapon and the head of the Empire himself were both in the same place. The Alliance took the bait.

ADMIRAL OZZEL

Admiral Ozzel was clumsy and stupid. He was also the Imperial Navy officer in command of the Imperial Death Squadron prior to the Battle of Hoth. Ozzel was a man of little imagination and worked by-the-manual, unable to cope with situations for which he had not been specifically trained. When Captain Piett reported signs of life in the Hoth system, Admiral Ozzel ignored him. Eventually, however, Darth Vader decided to investigate Piett's discoveries.

Ozzel brought the Imperial fleet out of hyperspace too close to the Hoth system and thus immediately alerted the Rebels to the imminent attack. Thanks to this display of incompetence, the Rebels were able to erect a protective energy shield over Echo Base preventing any Imperial bombardment.

What would have been a simple bombing strike now turned into a costly ground invasion. It was a serious mistake, and it was the last one Ozzel ever made. Using the Force, Vader telekinetically strangled Ozzel and placed Captain Piett in command of the fleet.

ADMIRAL CONAN ANTONIO MOTTI

Admiral Motti was the senior Imperial commander in charge of operations aboard the first Death Star. He was extremely arrogant and refused to believe that the battle station could be beaten by anything or anyone.

Motti believed in things that he could see and touch. He put his faith and trust in technology and science, and he found Darth Vader's devotion to the Force archaic and ridiculous. When Vader failed to produce the location of the main Rebel headquarters, Motti openly laughed at him. However, scoffing at the Dark Lord of the Sith was not a wise move. Vader inflicted a telekinetic stranglehold on the Admiral, showing him what powers he could command through the Force. Grand Moff Tarkin asked Vader to release Motti and the Sith lord complied, but Motti would not forget the lesson he had learned that day.

Motti died on board the Death Star when the Rebel Alliance pilot Luke Skywalker destroyed the 'indestructible' weapon.

ADMIRAL PIETT

Admiral Piett was an intelligent and loyal Imperial officer. He served faithfully aboard Darth Vader's flagship, the *Executor*, during the Hoth campaign. He was far more creative than his predecessor Admiral Ozzel, and he held the position of Admiral until the Battle of Endor. He was killed during the battle when a wayward A-wing starfighter crashed into the *Executor's* bridge, and therefore never saw the collapse of the Empire he had served for so long.

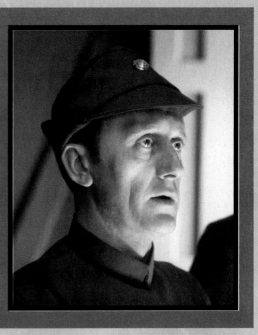

THE REBEL ALLIANCE

The Rebel Alliance spent long and painful years fighting against the Empire's stranglehold on the galaxy.

IDENTITY FILE

The Alliance began as a motley group of freedom fighters who were ill-equipped to challenge an enemy as mighty as the Galactic Empire. They were joined by senators like Bail Organa and Mon Mothma, who united the scattered resistance groups into the Rebel Alliance. Over the oppressive years of Imperial rule, they would work tirelessly to bring about the removal of the Emperor and the destruction of the Empire.

THE CORELLIAN TREATY

The Corellian Treaty marked the official formation of the Alliance. Three major Resistance groups agreed to ally with the Rebellion. They swore a solemn vow to fight either to the death, or to the end of the Empire. Mon Mothma was made supreme ruler of the Alliance, along with her Advisory Council. Far from the style of supreme rulership that Palpatine had grasped, Mon Mothma's continued role as leader was voted on every two years by Alliance representatives. However, she was never challenged.

The Corellian Treaty laid out the command structure of the Alliance and the roles of the allies. While each member was free to govern themselves and their territories, Mon Mothma and the Advisory Council was in command of supply, recruitment, training, inter-Ally communication, intelligence and all space operations.

The two main organisations that made up the Rebel Alliance were the Civil Government and the Military. The Civil Government handled supply, transport, taxation and diplomatic relations. The Military had command of the Alliance fleet and ground forces. Both branches were governed by Mon Mothma.

After the signing of the Corellian Treaty, scores of Rebel bases were established throughout the galaxy, with the Alliance High Command base constantly on the move. During the course of the Galactic Civil War, it inhabited bases on Dantooine, Yavin 4, Thila, Hoth, Golrath and Arbra as well as being posted with the fleet.

A MAJOR VICTORY

The first notable success for the Rebel Alliance came when they used stolen technical plans to formulate an attack strategy and destroy the Death Star. Incensed, the Emperor tasked Darth Vader with pursuing them more aggressively than ever before. During the next three years, the core group of Alliance commanders fled from base to base, constantly eluding the Empire's forces.

DID YOU KNOW?

There were many Rebel Alliance Sector Forces scattered throughout the galaxy. They drew the Empire's attention away from the activities of the core Rebels by carrying out many small attacks. In this way the Emperor's forces were spread thin and the Alliance had time to regroup and develop its final push against Palpatine.

THE EMPIRE UNDER THREAT

The Alliance had a central base on the ice planet of Hoth, but eventually Imperial probes discovered them. The High Command group escaped Darth Vader's clutches by the skin of their teeth and they were forced to evacuate. After the Battle of Hoth, the Rebel leaders stayed with the ever-mobile and always-growing Alliance Fleet.

At long last, about a year after the Battle of Hoth, the Rebellion was ready to make an all-out strike against the Empire. The opportunity came at the Battle of Endor. Even though they discovered that it was an Imperial trap, the Rebels did not give up. Through the bravery of the individual Rebels and their new allies, the Ewoks, he conflict ended with the death of Emperor Palpatine, the destruction of the second Death Star, the scattering of the Imperial Fleet and the end of the Empire's cruel regime.

MON MOTHMA

Mon Mothma was an influential loyalist Senator in the final days of the Galactic Republic. Together with Bail Organa, she was one of the first to be wary of Supreme Chancellor Palpatine's policies during the Clone Wars. When Palpatine created a new system whereby territorial governors reported directly to him, Mothma realised that the Senate was losing its last shreds of political influence. She began to organise intelligence cells, which were set up as pockets of resistance to challenge the Empire, each one unaware of the other cells' existence. When the Empire's outrages became too difficult to ignore, she helped to forge an Alliance of like-minded rebels that would eventually restore freedom to the galaxy.

Mon Mothma and Bail Organa were often opponents on the Senate floor, but they agreed that Palpatine had to be stopped. Together, they planned and carried out a plan for the Rebel Alliance. While Organa secretly helped the Alliance, he still played the role of political opponent to Mon Mothma.

When the Emperor decided to arrest Mothma, Organa informed her, allowing her to escape just in time. She spent the next few years on the run from the Empire. As a fugitive, she made contact with various resistance groups, trying to persuade them to join together. Her life was threatened not only by Imperial agents, but also by overly suspicious resistance groups.

As soon as the Alliance was truly formed, Mothma wrote the 'Declaration of Rebellion'. The document was issued publicly but it was personally addressed to Palpatine and accused him of a number of crimes. As a result of the declaration, many worlds decided to ally themselves with the Rebellion.

After the Rebel victory at Endor, Mothma was faced with the challenge of transforming the militarised Rebellion into a fully functional government. She rose to the challenge magnificently.

BIGGS DARKLIGHTER

Biggs Darklighter was a childhood friend of Luke Skywalker. The two grew up together on Tatooine and spent much of their reckless younger years speeding through Beggar's Canyon on their T-16 skyhoppers. They referred to themselves as a couple of 'shooting stars'.

Biggs parted from Luke when he joined the Imperial Academy. They had both longed to join up and Luke had been devastated when his uncle refused to allow him to. However, when Biggs returned from the Academy he was a changed man. He told Luke that about the true, evil nature of the Empire, and revealed that he had defected from the Empire to join the Rebel Alliance.

Biggs and Luke were reunited a short time later on the fourth moon of Yavin. They flew together in Red Squadron just as they had once flown through Beggar's Canyon. Their mission was to attack and destroy the Death Star that was approaching the Rebel base. Luke was successful in obliterating the Imperial battle station, but to his horror his friend Biggs was killed when Darth Vader shot his starfighter to pieces.

STORMTROOPERS

SPACETROOPERS

Spacetroopers were trained for exclusive space combat. They wore massive suits of armour, powered by servomotors. Each suit acted as a miniature spacecraft, with propulsion systems, sensor systems and weapons. In full gear, a spacetrooper stood over two meters tall and was twice as wide as an unarmoured soldier. The standard spacetrooper armour featured concussion grenades, mini proton-torpedo launchers, a blaster cannon and laser-cutters.

RADTROOPERS

Radiation zone assault troops were trained to handle irradiated combat zones. Their heavy armour featured a lead-polymer substrate and had a silvery reflective finish.

IDENTITY FILE

Stormtroopers were elite shock troops who were fanatically loyal to the Empire and impossible to sway from the Imperial cause. They wore intimidating white armour, which incorporated a wide range of survival equipment and temperature controls. These enabled the soldiers to survive in almost any environment. Stormtroopers used blaster rifles and pistols, and attacked in hordes to overwhelm their enemies. Along with standard stormtroopers, the Empire also organised several specialised units. Truly elite stormtroopers could be selected to join the Emperor's Royal Guard. Stormtroopers were in service aboard all Imperial vessels and were used as first-strike forces in most conflicts. Garrisons of stormtroopers were also stationed on worlds throughout the galaxy to crush uprisings and make sure that people and governments did as they were told. The stormtroopers could not be bribed and were completely under the Emperor's command. Because of this, they also policed the Imperial officers, making sure that no one was preparing to betray the Emperor.

DID YOU KNOW?

After the Emperor's death, stormtroopers remained a major component of the Imperial army and were instrumental in the schemes of Grand Admiral Thrawn and other villains.

Clone scouts had wiry builds and smaller bones than standard stormtrooper clones. A newer batch of clones had blond hair while an earlier batch had sleek black hair.

Stormtrooper training was so effective that individuals would obey their officers without question and without regard to the rights of others or even to their own safety.

Rocket troopers wore powersuits equipped with jetpacks. Hazard troopers wore powersuits suits for harsh environments.

Stormtrooper unit organisation was separate to that of the Imperial Army and Navy. They followed similar organisation patterns: squads, platoons, companies, battalions, regiments and battlegroups (called legions). A stormtrooper battalion had 820 men.

SNOWTROOPERS

Snowtroopers wore customised armour that was carefully designed to withstand the climate extremes of ice planets such as Hoth. Their suits incorporated fabric overgarments that helped contain heat, and terrain-gripping boots to combat slippery conditions. Each suit of armour included a more powerful heating unit and a breather hood covered the faceplate and fed into the suit liner.

TECHNOLOGICAL PROTECTION

A standard stormtrooper suit consisted of 18 individual pieces of hardened plastoid composite armour over a black body glove. These suits had temperature controls and built-in life-support systems, allowing stormtroopers to brave a wide range of hostile environments. The armour also provided limited protection from blaster fire. Stormtrooper armour could be sealed and had a self-contained air supply, allowing the wearer to survive in the vacuum of space for brief periods of time.

A stormtrooper's helmet was equipped with polarised lenses, transmitters and sensor arrays. The utility belt contained emergency batteries, extra ammunition and a grappling hook. On the back of the belt was a thermal detonator with unlabelled code keys.

SEATROOPERS

Seatroopers were trained to operate in marine environments. They had modified scout armour with breathing tanks, flippers and a helmet-mounted spotlight. They operated patrol vehicles such as waveskimmers and wavespeeders.

SAND TROOPERS

Although their armour resembled that of a standard stormtrooper, sandtroopers were equipped with modified armour and gear to better withstand missions in harsh, desert locations. The advanced cooling systems in their helmets and suits gave these troopers protection from the relentless heat.

The stormtrooper detachment that was sent by Darth Vader to investigate a crashed escape pod on Tatooine consisted of sandtroopers. They had heavy weapons, survival gear and shoulder badges denoting rank.

GRAND MOFF TARKIN

The Death Star project was Tarkin's brainchild. To him, people were just commodities and their lives were unimportant.

Grand Moff Tarkin was cold and calculating, with more than a streak of sadism about his personality.

IDENTITY FILE

Grand Moff Tarkin was the Imperial governor of the Outland Regions, and he masterminded the Death Star project. He was a gifted but ruthless tactician and a loyal believer in Emperor Palpatine's vision of the New Order. He thought that the power of the battle station's prime weapon was enough to deter any rebellion. Palpatine liked the way Tarkin thought, and promoted him to an important position within the Empire.

GREAT AMBITIONS

As a young man, Wilhuff Tarkin had visions of a brighter and better future. From his home on Eriadu, a densely populated world in the Seswenna sector, he saw the decay inherent in the Republic. Tarkin climbed up through the military and political ranks of Eriadu, always aiming for something higher. During the last days of the Republic, he made valuable contacts in Palpatine's Senate, and in the world of big business.

THE GHORMAN MASSACRE

Not long after Palpatine restructured the galactic government, Tarkin orchestrated a terrible outrage on the distant world of Ghorman. Hundreds of activists were on a landing platform, protesting about Imperial taxation. Tarkin landed his vessel on top of them. Instead of receiving a punishment for this crime, was rewarded with command of the Seswenna sector.

To demonstrate the Death Star's power, Tarkin destroyed the planet of Alderaan in front of its horrified princess, Leia.

GRAND MOFF

Tarkin knew that the resistance forces took advantage of the bureaucratic borders that separated sectors, knowing that they could elude Imperial sector forces by jumping out of their spheres of influence. To prevent this, he proposed a new organisational scheme to the Emperor. In addition to the sectors defined by astrographic and political boundaries, he recommended overlapping 'priority sectors'. These sectors would be defined by the amount of treasonous activity therein. A single official would command these territories - a Grand Moff - and he would oversee the allotment of resources personally. Palpatine was pleased with Tarkin's proposal, and granted Tarkin the title and an enormous area of operations in the Outer Rim Territories.

THE TARKIN DOCTRINE

Another of Tarkin's innovations was the so-called doctrine of fear, or the Tarkin Doctrine as it was officially known. It would have taken incredible amounts of resources to completely dominate all the worlds of the Empire. Tarkin suggested that instead, the New Order should carry out a single show of force so terrifying in its power that it would put an end to any treasonous activity.

Palpatine liked this idea, and this was the beginning of the creation of the Death Star, which was another of Tarkin's brilliant visions. A selection of advanced scientists in a secret laboratory known as Maw Installation made this vision a reality.

THE DEATH STAR

Tarkin's creation was intended to strike fear into the hearts of every citizen of the galaxy, but ultimately it was a place of death and destruction for its creator. When Luke Skywalker fired a proton torpedo volley into a weak spot in the battle station, the mighty weapon exploded and Tarkin was killed.

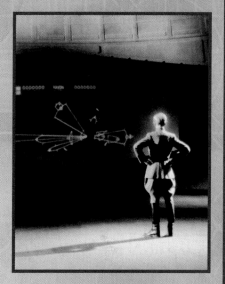

JAWAS

SAND SURVIVAL

A desert planet such as Tatooine did not provide an easy lifestyle for its inhabitants. Over the years, Jawas evolved several extremely important survival traits. They had exceptional night vision, a strong immune system and an efficient digestive system that drew all the nutrients they needed from their simple diet of hubba gourd.

The Jawas travelled around in enormous vehicles called sandcrawlers, which contained warren-like compartments and large storage areas for all the scrap they scavenged.

IDENTITY FILE

The Jawas lived on the desert planet of Tatooine, and they posed a great danger to any hapless droid that crossed their path. Many dangers lurked among the dunes and crags of Tatooine's dry plains, but few could affect a droid's behavioral matrix circuitry like the Jawas.

The Jawas were scavengers. They travelled across the deserts of Tatooine looking for discarded scrap metal and lost droids. They had some simple weaponry that they had cobbled together from what they could find, and they used it to incapacitate droids. The droids would then find themselves inside the Jawa's fortress-like sandcrawler homes.

The Jawas refurbished their finds as quickly as they could and went on to sell them to moisture farmers, who found it difficult to find a better selection elsewhere. Their work was shoddy and haphazard, and the colonists on Tatooine knew that the Jawas would hoodwink them if they could.

Despite their reputation, Jawas were an important part of the circle of trade that connected the communities on Tatooine. Moisture farms and small communities were spread far apart across the deserts and they were often forced to rely upon the Jawas to provide them with much-needed equipment.

A REPUGNANT STENCH

What lay beneath a Jawa's mask was ugly and repulsive, and rarely seen by outsiders. Their faces were permanently obscured by clouds of insects that gathered in the recesses and folds of their cowls, attracted by their foul stench. The particular odour that emanated from a Jawa was a combination of poor hygiene and a solution into which they dipped their clothes to retain moisture. The odour told other Jawas a wealth of information, such as clan lineage, health, emotional state and even the last meal eaten.

The droids C-3PO and R2-D2 were captured by Jawas after they escaped Darth Vader and his stormtroopers. They were sold to Owen Lars, who asked his nephew Luke to check them over.

Jawas were humanoids and stood at about one metre tall. They kept themselves completely hidden behind rough, hand-woven robes. Large hoods concealed their faces, and the only parts of a Jawa that could be seen were its glowing yellow eyes.

SCAVENGING FOR A LIVING

The Dune Sea was littered with derelict spacecraft wreckage from millennia of star travel. This bounty of rubbish had inspired the Jawas to become scavengers, and after many generations they were highly skilled at their work. They built homes and tools from the ancient scraps they discovered. Even their sandcrawlers were scavenged – they were cast-off mobile smelters from failed outlander mining attempts.

JAWA SOCIETY

Jawas lived in family clans, and each clan had a distinct territory for living and scavenging. Half the clan spent its time in the compartments of a sandcrawler, scouring the deserts for usable salvage. The other half lived inside a thick-walled fortress. The Jawas built these strongholds to protect themselves from Tusken Raiders and krayt dragons.

A chief led each clan and the chiefs were usually male. In Jawa society, females were seen as second-class citizens at best, and property at worst. However, one type of female in Jawa culture commanded great respect: the shamans.

A Jawa would become a shaman when she was afflicted by an illness that gave her a hallucinatory vision. She would be declared a shaman depending on the outcome of the vision – and if she survived her illness. Shamans were seen as very wise and were given respect accordingly.

THE GREAT SWAP MEET

Once a year, the scattered Jawa clans gathered in one place for the great swap meet. All the sandcrawlers would converge and the Jawas would exchange salvage. Jawa children and females were also exchanged between clans and marriages were arranged.

SEE-THREEPIO AND ARTOO-DETOO

Jawas played a small but important role in the collapse of the Empire. They captured the droids R2-D2 and C-3PO when they arrived on Tatooine to search for Obi-Wan Kenobi. The Jawas then sold the droids to Luke Skywalker's family, and this was the beginning of Luke's adventures. Skywalker would go on to liberate the galaxy from the clutches of the twisted Emperor Palpatine.

Luke Skywalker

IDENTITY FILE

Luke Skywalker was raised by his uncle, Owen Lars, and his aunt, Beru, on their moisture farm in a remote part of Tatooine. He was the son of Anakin Skywalker and Senator Padmé Amidala. When his mother died in childbirth, he and his twin sister, Leia were hidden from their father, who had been seduced by the dark side of the Force. Luke was taken to Tatooine by Obi-Wan Kenobi and entrusted into the care of his uncle. Obi-Wan lived as a recluse nearby to keep watch over the boy and meditate on the Force.

As a young man Luke was orphaned when Imperial stormtroopers razed his home to the ground and murdered his aunt and uncle. The stormtroopers were looking for the droids that they had tracked to the Lars farm, R2-D2 and C-3PO, understood to have been carrying sensitive Imperial plans. Luke pledged himself to becoming a Jedi and he, Obi-Wan and the droids left on a mission of utmost importance.

Luke did not know that he had a sister, but they became good friends before they learned of their shared heritage. Luke became a highly regarded pilot in the Rebel Alliance and a very powerful Jedi. He brought about the end of the Empire and turned his father from the dark side of the Force.

Luke was trained to feel the Force flow through him, and to recognise the Force all around him. Obi-Wan was preparing Luke for a destiny that he could never have imagined and trying to teach him the patience that his father lacked.

JEDI TRAINING

Luke's Jedi training was improvised by Obi-Wan Kenobi. In the old days of the Republic he would never have been trained because of his age. However, there was little hope for the galaxy without Skywalker. Although Obi-Wan never told him the whole truth, Luke learned that his father was once a great and powerful Jedi. Obi-Wan gave Luke Anakin's lightsaber, which he had lost on Mustafar during their great duel.

With lightsaber in hand, Luke began on a journey that would see him become one of the greatest Jedi of all time. Obi-Wan tried to teach him the discipline and patience that Anakin had lacked. When the time came, Obi-Wan allowed himself to be slain by Darth Vader, although he continued to communicate with Luke through the Force.

Luke's expertise in the Force grew until Obi-Wan appeared to him on the ice planet Hoth and instructed him to seek out Yoda. In the swamps of Dagobah, Yoda taught Luke the secrets of the Force, testing his patience, his belief and his emotional detachment. Luke was too headstrong and, although he had made progress, he failed the tests and set off to face Vader before he was ready.

Darth Vader defeated the young Jedi and revealed that he was Luke's father. Luke travelled to Tatooine to construct a new lightsaber and rescue his friend Han Solo from the clutches of Jabba the Hutt. He returned to Dagobah to complete his training only to find Yoda on his deathbed. His training required but one more task. He would have to face Vader once more; only then would he become a Jedi.

Luke gave himself up to Darth Vader and was taken before the Emperor, yet he had sensed a conflict inside his father. The Emperor pitted father and son against each other in the hope that Luke would kill his father and become a Sith Lord. Although Luke nearly succumbed to the dark side and in a fit of rage severely wounded his father, he re-focused himself and refused to kill him. Luke's compassion saved him and his Jedi training was complete.

"I'LL NEVER TURN TO THE DARK SIDE... I AM A JEDI, LIKE MY FATHER BEFORE ME."

Although tempted by the Vader and dark side of the Force, Luke resisted and was almost killed. In the future, he would see similarities between himself and Vader and use them to make the right choices.

FROM BEGGARS CANYON TO THE DEATH STAR

Luke was an ace pilot as a child and used to practice flying through Beggars Canyon on Tatooine with his friend Biggs Darklighter. The T-16 Skyhopper was similar to the T-65 X-wing starfighters, so Luke had the all the right training. Coupled with his training in the Force, he became a legendary pilot.

During the Battle of Yavin it was Luke who had the nerve to release his proton torpedoes at just the right second to destroy the Death Star. He had turned off his targeting computer before making the shot and used the Force to guide him.

Luke became a commander in the Rebel Alliance and led Rogue Group's snowspeeders as they fought against the Imperial ground troops on Hoth. They gave the Rebel fleet enough time to escape the invasion and jump to a rendezvous point far away from Darth Vader.

Luke longed for excitement and adventure, yet he was stuck working on his uncle's farm on Tatooine. His uncle did not want him to get involved in the war against the Empire.

ENDANGERING THE MISSION

Before the Battle of Endor a Rebel strike team was sent to the surface of the Sanctuary Moon with the task of destroying the shield generator. With the shield destroyed the incomplete Death Star would be vulnerable to an attack. The team was led by Han Solo and included Leia, Chewbacca, C-3PO and R2-D2. At the last minute Luke also volunteered himself onto the team.

As the Rebels advanced, Luke could sense Vader's presence on the battle station and realised that he had put the mission in jeopardy. Vader sensed Luke also, and allowed the Rebels to make it to the surface of the moon so that he could deal with them himself. After Luke had befriended the Ewoks, he left to confront Vader, but not before he revealed to Leia that she was his sister.

Luke gave himself up at the Imperial base and Vader was there personally to escort him to the Emperor's throne room aboard the Death Star. Luke did not know that he was falling into another one of Palpatine's twisted plans. However, Luke had sensed the good in Vader and this spurred him on to fulfil his destiny.

PRINCESS LEIA ORGANA

Although they infuriated each other, romantic sparks flew between Princess Leia and Han Solo.

IDENTITY FILE

Leia was the twin sister of Luke Skywalker, separated from him at birth to keep her safe from Emperor Palpatine and Darth Vader. Leia was entrusted to Bail Organa, the Viceroy and First Chairman of the planet Alderaan. She was raised by Organa and his wife as their adopted child and followed in the footsteps of her 'father' when she entered into politics. Leia became the youngest member of the Imperial Senate.

Leia's political loyalties were secretly devoted to the Rebel Alliance, and she used her diplomatic immunity to carry supplies and information for the Rebels. Leia was a skilled diplomat and a bold and decisive leader. When she later became a full-time member and leader of the Rebel Alliance, she was involved in several key battles. She had command decisions in many military exercises that helped bring about the end of the Empire.

TRAITOR!

As an Imperial Senator, Leia used her diplomatic immunity to aid the Rebel Cause. Travelling in her recognised consular ship, *Tantive IV*, she intercepted some technical read-outs stolen by Rebel spies. These plans showed the blueprints of the Imperial Death Star, a new and devastating weapon that was the size of a small moon. Leia's mission was to take these plans to Obi-Wan Kenobi and bring him to Alderaan to meet with her father and advise the Alliance.

En route to Tatooine, *Tantive IV* was attacked and boarded by Imperial forces led by Darth Vader himself. Accused of spying, Leia was taken prisoner by Vader and transported to the Death Star. Vader tortured Leia with his mind probes, but she showed considerable resistance to his methods. Vader then brought Leia before Grand Moff Tarkin. Leia told Tarkin a lie, which he believed, about the location of the Rebel base. However, he still destroyed her home world before her eyes.

Back in her cell Leia awaited execution, but Luke Skywalker and Han Solo rescued her. Together with Chewbacca, R2 and C-3PO they escaped the Death Star, but not before witnessing the murder of Obi-Wan by Darth Vader. The plans were still safe aboard Artoo and Leia directed the *Falcon* to the real Rebel base on Yavin 4.

Vader had placed a homing device on board the *Millennium Falcon* and the Death Star followed them to Yavin 4. With just enough time to prepare, the Rebels were able to destroy the Death Star, owing to the courage and ingenuity Leia showed upon her capture.

Princess Leia was the daughter of Padmé Amidala and Anakin Skywalker, and Luke's twin sister. Although she did not know her true identity, she grew up as a strong-minded and independent person and was determined to release the galaxy from the Emperor's evil control.

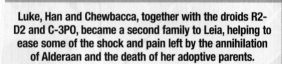

Luke, Han and Chewbacca, together with the droids R2-D2 and C-3PO, became a second family to Leia, helping to ease some of the shock and pain left by the annihilation of Alderaan and the death of her adoptive parents.

LOVE AND HATE

Leia first met Han Solo when he partnered with Luke Skywalker for her rescue. Han was attracted to the task owing to Leia's presumed wealth; she was, after all, a princess. From the moment they laid eyes on each other sparks began to fly. She thought him arrogant, and he found her ungrateful. However, with their rescue attempt failing, Leia ordered Luke, Han and Chewbacca into the garbage chute and effectively saved them all.

After the Battle of Yavin, Leia became a full-time member of the Rebel Alliance, often acting as a diplomat to get other worlds to join the fight against the Empire. At first she displayed overt hostility towards Han and he responded in kind. However, at quiet moments they were drawn to each other and Han made his moves.

Leia and Han fell in love but they had no time to cement it, as they were on the run from Darth Vader. Captured by the Sith lord, Leia managed to tell Han 'I love you' only seconds before he was encased in carbonite.

Leia entered the palace of Jabba the Hutt in the disguise of the bounty hunter Boushh. She had Chewbacca in tow. She managed to free Han from his carbonite block, but Jabba discovered her and forced her to join his court as a prisoner and to wear a dancing girl's outfit. She eventually killed Jabba by strangling him with the very chain that bound her. Skywalker triggered a rescue that resulted in the destruction of Jabba's sail barge and the death of many of his henchmen.

After a daring rescue in the heart of Jabba the Hutt's palace, Leia and Han were reunited. She had endured humiliation and risked her life to save him. However, they had an Empire to destroy and there was no time to waste. Together they led a strike team on the forest moon of Endor, their mission to destroy the generator that powered the protective shield around the second Death Star. With the help of the Ewoks the second battle station was destroyed. At last the galaxy was free and Leia and Han were finally able to declare their true feelings for one another.

DID YOU KNOW?

Leia encountered Vader on the planet Mimban, where he badly wounded her with his lightsaber. Luke managed to drive off Vader and help heal Leia through the powers of the Kaiburr Crystal.

DAUGHTER OF SKYWALKER

When Leia was first captured and tortured by Darth Vader, neither of them had an inkling of the relationship that truly linked them. The truth was that she and Luke were twins, and their father had been the famous Jedi Knight Anakin Skywalker. When he was seduced by the dark side of the Force, he had become Darth Vader. When Luke told her the truth on the forest moon of Endor, Leia began to understand that many things she had attributed to intuition had really been the glimmerings of untrained Jedi abilities.

HAN SOLO

Han Solo was born on Corellia and worked as a smuggler. He was a quick-talking, quick-thinking and charming rogue, whose life had been spent getting in and out of trouble. His experiences had taught him to be suspicious of everyone and to value money above all else, but his true nature was warm and loyal, and he would have laid down his life for his friends. His early years could never have prepared him for the fact that he would one day become one of the heroes of the Rebel Alliance.

Han Solo was a scoundrel and a smuggler whose life was turned upside down when he met Jedi Master Obi-Wan Kenobi and young Luke Skywalker.

CHEWBACCA

Solo enrolled in the Imperial Academy, but his stubborn nature and belief in fairness soon got him into trouble. He interfered with some slavers who were mistreating an enslaved Wookiee and for his insubordination he was discharged. The Wookiee he rescued, Chewbacca, stayed with him, at first to pay him back for the rescue and then as his partner and friend.

THE *MILLENNIUM FALCON*

Solo won a Corellian light freighter, the *Millennium Falcon*, from gambling buddy Lando Calrissian. The ship looked like a bucket of bolts, but Solo and Chewbacca modified it into one of the fastest starships in the galaxy.

DID YOU KNOW?

Solo's earliest memory was of begging on the streets of Corellia. He was at least five years old at the time.

The scar on his chin marks a wound he received during a tangle with a knife-wielding shore-gang chief.

Han spent most of his childhood in the service of Garris Shrike, the leader of a trading clan that used abandoned street urchins as beggars and petty thieves. He grew up on Shrike's ship, the *Trader's Luck*, and was mostly raised by a kind female Wookiee named Dewlanna, who taught him compassion and the Wookiee language.

Princess Leia was the love of Han Solo's life, but he found it hard to put down his well-developed guard of arrogance and sarcasm. Even when he was about to be encased in carbonite and Leia told him that she loved him, his only response was: "I know."

THE HERO OF YAVIN

To earn money, Solo took on mercenary jobs and ran a regular glitterstim spice smuggling route for the likes of criminal kingpin Jabba the Hutt. On one such mission, Solo was boarded by Imperial customs officials and had to dump the spice. The furious Jabba demanded repayment, so Solo agreed to take some passengers to Alderaan for a large fee. Before he knew it, he was at the heart of the Rebellion.

Against his better judgment, and complaining loudly, Solo helped rescue the beautiful Princess Leia Organa from a prison cell aboard the Imperial Death Star. Later, after claiming he was leaving to pay off Jabba, he returned in the *Falcon* just in time to help Luke destroy the Death Star. He was known as one of the Heroes of Yavin for the part he played in this first decisive victory for the Rebels.

Despite promising skills that he developed as a teenage swoop racer, Solo was drummed out of the Imperial Navy when he defied orders and rescued a Wookiee slave, Chewbacca.

PIRATES!

After the Death Star crisis, Solo and Chewbacca left the Rebel base to pay off their debt to Jabba the Hutt. However, en route to Tatooine the *Millennium Falcon* was attacked by a pirate force commanded by Crimson Jack. The pirate robbed Solo of his reward money and the two smugglers had no option but to return to the Rebel fold.

JABBA'S REVENGE

Solo spent the next three years helping the Alliance, during which time his feelings for Princess Leia grew and deepened, although their relationship was always explosive. Uncomfortable with baring his soul, Solo hid his true attraction to Leia under a façade of arrogant bravado that infuriated her.

By the time Solo decided to return to Tatooine to pay his debt, Jabba had already put a price on his head, and a swathe of bounty hunters were tracking him down. Eventually, Boba Fett tracked him to Cloud City, where Darth Vader set a trap to capture him.

Vader had Solo encased in carbonite, then gave him to Fett to transport to Jabba. The Hutt lord hung him on the wall as if he were a piece of artwork, determined to keep him there as a warning to others who tried to cross him. However, Solo's friends were determined to rescue him. They infiltrated Jabba's palace and carried out a rescue that led to the death of the repulsive Jabba.

THE END OF IMPERIAL RULE

Solo went on to lead a strike force to the forest moon of Endor. The mission was vital - they had to disable a defensive shield that protected the Empire's second Death Star. With the help of the native Ewoks, Solo succeeded at the last possible moment. As the galaxy celebrated its freedom, Han at last declared his true feelings for Princess Leia. Together, they would form a core part of the new Galactic Republic.

MOS EISLEY

IDENTITY FILE

It was common knowledge that Mos Eisley was a pirate city. One of the largest spaceports on Tatooine, it was arranged in a wheel formation, with the central power and water distribution plants at its centre. Circular docking bays and landing pads dotted the city, and the sky was busy with interstellar traffic.

Mos Eisley Spaceport began as an alternative to the then-bustling Anchorhead port, which many residents found too expensive. Rodian refugees helped with the building and their hard work created a city. However, their corrupt lives also brought vice and crime to the port.

RECKLESS CRIMINALS

Although it was not the capital city, Mos Eisley's prominence in Tatooine's trade and tourism industries gave it high status. Even the crime lord Jabba the Hutt moved some of his operations to a house in the downtown area. The city was riddled by criminal transients and it was the place Obi-Wan Kenobi and Luke Skywalker went to find a pilot reckless enough to take them off Tatooine. They met Han Solo and Chewbacca in the Cantina and persuaded the two smugglers to take them as passengers.

CITY LAYOUT

Mos Eisley was divided into a 'New Quarter' and an 'Old Quarter'. The Old Quarter was the area that attracted the most dubious characters. It was here that Jabba maintained his residence and it was also home to the infamous Mos Eisley Cantina. The Cantina was owned by a Wookiee called Chalmun, and it regularly played host to some of the most dangerous and bizarre criminals in the galaxy.

The New Quarter was more of a tourist area. It contained a (legal) merchant district and plenty of places for tourists to relax. However, even here one only had to scratch the surface to discover the grey and black markets beneath.

THE CANTINA

Looking at the exterior of the Mos Eisley Cantina, no one would have suspected how many strange and scary aliens were within seeking shade, business and refreshment. The cantina was carefully designed according to its clientele. Upon first entering the establishment, a patron would step into a darkened alcove. The time it took for the newcomer's eyes to adjust to the shadows gave the bar just enough time to check out the new arrival.

The main room contained a scattering of booths and free-standing tables. An all-alien band played a lively tune in the corner, and a gruff bartender concocted exotic mixtures from behind the bar. There were only two rules in the cantina; droids were not allowed inside, and if anyone got involved in a dispute, they had to leave blasters out of it. All sorts of underhand and illegal deals were made in the Cantina's shadowy corners.

MODAL NODES

The seven-member Cantina band was made up of Bith aliens playing a variety of wind and percussion instruments. These were the Modal Nodes, who were trained in jazzy popular music. The frontman was Fiery Figrin D'an, who was a card-shark and an expert on the kloo horn and the gasan string drum. Backing him up on wind instruments were Doikk Na'ts on the Dorenian Beshniquel, and Ickabel G'ont and Tedn Dahai on their fanfars. Tech Mo'r rounded out the band on the Ommni Box and Nalan Cheel played the horn bell-bedecked bandfill. Lirin Car'n only sat in from time to time, but he played a mean kloo horn backup.

The Bith were naturally laid-back and thoughtful beings, but sometimes Figrin's habit of compulsively gambling away their earnings (and their instruments) would inflame the passions of the other band members. Being plunged into some of the seamiest and most unsavoury venues in the galaxy did not help.

The band was popular and talented; they appealed to Jabba the Hutt and became his house band … until his fickle tastes turned. As soon as they got the chance, they fled from Tatooine to continue pursuing fame and fortune through the galaxy.

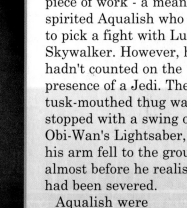

PONDA BABA

Ponda Baba was a nasty piece of work - a mean-spirited Aqualish who tried to pick a fight with Luke Skywalker. However, he hadn't counted on the presence of a Jedi. The tusk-mouthed thug was stopped with a swing of Obi-Wan's Lightsaber, and his arm fell to the ground almost before he realised it had been severed.

Aqualish were notoriously bad tempered, and Ponda Baba was no exception. He was a pirate and smuggler who worked in partnership with a homicidal maniac called Dr Evazan. The doctor used his questionable medical skills to tend to Baba's wounds, but he botched the surgery and they fell out. Baba tried to track down Evazan to wreak revenge, but they managed to put aside their differences and teamed up again.

THE CANTINA ALIENS

The Cantina regulars came from every planet and walk of life, and when Luke Skywalker first entered the bar he was flabbergasted; he had never seen so many aliens together at the same time.

HAMMERHEADS

Hammerheads were tall, gentle herbivores from the planet Ithor. Ithorians got their nickname thanks to their most prominent feature: a long, curving neck ending in a t-shaped dome of a head. On the sides of their curling necks, Ithorians had two mouths. This created a disconcerting stereo effect when they spoke.

Ithorians worshipped the 'Mother Jungle'; a spirit who was the embodiment of the lush, tropical ecology of their world. However, most Ithorians never set foot on their own planet. They lived in floating cities above the surface, and only three of their continents had been developed; the other two had never been touched by Ithorian hands.

The inhabitants of Ithor were peace-loving and devoted much time to thinking about their ecology, and respecting all living things. They were also extremely curious and outgoing, and many found their way to the stars to explore some of the galaxy around them. They had 'herd ships' that resembled their floating cities, and these had complex life-support systems that replicated the environment of Ithor, complete with jungles, wildlife and even weather patterns.

JABBA THE HUTT

Jabba's palace was a fetid, immoral den of iniquity. He used people like possessions and drew sadistic pleasure from the pain and suffering of others.

The abhorrent crime lord Jabba the Hutt controlled a vast network of illegal activities that made him one of the wealthiest beings in the galaxy.

DID YOU KNOW?

Jabba had a tattoo of yoro root pigment.

His full name was Jabba Desilijic Tiure.

For the sake of his business interests, he was on the side of the Republic during the Clone Wars against rival Boorka the Hutt.

IDENTITY FILE

Jabba was a Hutt gangster who lived on Tatooine and had collected a fortune through his innumerable illegal activities. Jabba controlled the majority of the planet's cities, towns and spaceports. From his desert palace on Tatooine he ruled a criminal empire. His empire spanned a vast range of criminal activities, including piracy, slavery, gambling and the sale of stolen goods.

The son of a major clan leader and member of a long line of criminal masterminds, Jabba's ambition was to become his father's equal. By the time he was 600 years old, he had created a major criminal empire. The decadence of his palace attracted the scum of the galaxy, who flocked there for drink, food, entertainment and employment. Thieves, smugglers, assassins, spies, and all manner of criminals were constantly at Jabba's side.

The Hutt was involved in every kind of illicit enterprise in the Outer Rim, including smuggling, glitterstim spice dealing, slave trading, assassination, loan sharking, protection and piracy.

THE FACE OF CRIME

Jabba was physically repulsive. He looked like an obese slug and his legless, tapered body was coated in slime. A wide, drooling, toothless grin split his flat face, and two yellow-red snake-like eyes glinted from his immense head.

His depravity was legendary. His idea of entertainment was torturing and humiliating his subjects. He kept scantily clad slave girls chained to his throne for his amusement. In certain moods, Jabba enjoyed sending his possessions to gory deaths. The beautiful Twi'lek slave Oola was fed to the rancor beast that Jabba kept below his throne room.

Jabba met his end at the hands of Princess Leia, who he was holding captive as a slave girl. He would not live to regret mistreating the daughter of Padmé Amidala and Anakin Skywalker.

RISE OF A CRIMINAL MASTERMIND

Jabba inherited a great deal of wealth from his father Zorba, who was constantly in and out of prison. However, most of Jabba's fortune was earned through his myriad criminal activities. Jabba was the Hutt to be reckoned with, and his cunning and deceptiveness was legendary. For example, when he chose to hire Gamorreans as his guards, he had to follow Gamorrean tradition and defeat the pig-like warriors in combat. Knowing that he could not defeat a dozen of them at once, Jabba challenged them to blindfolded combat. Once the Gamorreans were blindfolded, 20 of Jabba's armed henchmen carried out a brutal attack on them. When the blindfolds were removed, Jabba claimed victory. The Gamorreans served him loyally ever after.

A THORN IN JABBA'S SIDE

When Jabba hired Han Solo to smuggle glitterstim spice from mines below the Imperial Correction Facility on Kessel, he set in motion a chain of events that would end in his own destruction. Solo was forced to jettison a glitterstim load to avoid Imperial entanglements, and Jabba sent out several bounty hunters in search of the smuggler.

Solo killed Greedo, one of Jabba's bounty hunters, but could not escape the Hutt. Jabba allowed him to transport passengers to Alderaan in exchange for the proceeds from the charter. Solo never returned. The incensed Jabba posted a huge reward for the smuggler's death or capture.

Eventually, Boba Fett delivered Solo, alive but frozen in a block of carbonite. The extraordinary pilot, smuggler and soldier was now little more than wall decoration for a grotesque crime lord.

JABBA'S LAST CHANCE

Solo's friends developed an elaborate plan to rescue him. They entered the palace and at first tried to bring a peaceful end to the situation. But Jabba captured Princess Leia and placed her in chains, then tried to feed Luke Skywalker to his pet rancor, and later the sarlacc. The Hutt had signed his own death warrant.

To Jabba's fury and astonishment, Luke used his Jedi powers to escape his fate. A mighty fight erupted between the Rebels and Jabba's men. During the fray, the livid Princess Leia got her revenge and used the chain that bound her to strangle her captor. Moments later, the rest of his court died horribly when Leia and Luke caused the sail barge to explode. Jabba's loathsome body was consumed in the flames.

LANDO CALRISSIAN

Lando Calrissian was cut from the same cloth as Han Solo; they were both pirates who relied on quick thinking and even quicker getaways.

IDENTITY FILE

Lando Calrissian was the suave and sophisticated baron-administrator of Bespin's Cloud City. A gambler, a businessman, some would even say an entrepreneur, Calrissian liked to ride his luck any way he could. A long-time associate of Han Solo, the two of them had a chequered past together. The main bone of contention was the ownership of the *Millennium Falcon*. The ship had passed between them over several games of sabacc, and Han won the ship in the end (although Lando maintained that he cheated).

Lando had turned his back on smuggling and made the transition from pirate to legitimate businessman. He led a comfortable life until the Empire showed up with an uncompromising deal, forcing him to betray Han Solo.

As roguish as Han Solo but possibly even more charming, Lando may have been a scoundrel but he had the heart of a hero. After betraying his friend he spent a long time putting things right and he was instrumental in the rescue of Han Solo from Jabba's palace. He joined the Rebel Alliance and his leadership qualities saw him receive the rank of General. It was he who volunteered to lead the Rebel fleet against the second Death Star at the Battle of Endor.

NO DEAL IS WORTH THIS

Soon after the Battle of Hoth, Darth Vader and Boba Fett arrived at Cloud City with a deal to assure the continued independence of the city. However, Lando would have to give up his friend Han Solo to Boba Fett. Seeing no other alternative, Lando agreed to sacrifice his friend for the sake of the people of Cloud City.

Once Vader had what he wanted, he changed the deal. Lando realised that he had been set up. He freed Leia and Chewbacca and vowed to rescue Han. He alerted the citizens of Cloud City to their imminent danger from the Empire before he set off on another adventure on the wrong side of the law.

Lando, Leia, Chewbacca, C-3PO and R2-D2 escaped Bespin in the *Millennium Falcon*, but Leia ordered the ship back to Cloud City where they rescued a near-dead Luke Skywalker.

In order to protect Cloud City, Lando was forced to make an agreement to deliver Han Solo and Leia to Darth Vader. As Vader renegotiated terms, Lando realised the deal had turned sour.

A HEROIC RESCUE

Once a plan was formed to rescue Han Solo, Calrissian infiltrated the palace of Jabba the Hutt on the remote planet of Tatooine. Dressed as a skiff guard, Lando lay in wait for Luke Skywalker, now a highly skilled near-Jedi, to carry out the plan.

One by one Leia, Chewbacca, R2-D2, C-3PO and Luke arrived. After freeing Han from the carbonite, Leia was discovered and had to suffer the indignity of becoming one of Jabba's slave girls. Chewbacca was also held prisoner.

When Skywalker arrived he used his considerable Force powers to gain entry to Jabba's Palace and inner sanctum. Jabba thought himself more than a match for the Jedi and sentenced him to death with Han and Chewbacca.

As they hovered over the Sarlacc pit, Luke gave the signal and Lando freed Han and Chewbacca as Luke fought off the other skiff guards. Leia throttled Jabba with the very chain with which she was being held and Luke rescued her from the main barge. Lando steered the skiff away, making sure that he picked up the two droids before Jabba's barge exploded.

GENERAL CALRISSIAN

On hearing of Lando's piloting prowess and his heroics in the rescue of Han Solo, the Rebel Alliance gave him the commission of General. He volunteered to lead the attack against the Death Star being built near Endor. Lando took over the *Millennium Falcon* and commanded the Rebel starfighters as Gold Leader.

With his co-pilot, a Sullustan by the name of Nien Nunb, General Calrissian headed for the Death Star. His gambler's instincts served him well as the Rebels soon became aware that they had been lured into a trap. Lando's tactics ensured the survival of the fleet until Han could destroy the shield generator.

With the shields down, Lando raced the *Millennium Falcon* to the heart of the Death Star and released several concussion missiles into the core reactor. As he turned the ship around, the explosion followed him and very nearly engulfed the *Falcon* in flames. Lando managed to outrun the fireball and turned back to see the Death Star destroyed. Lando was a hero and the Empire was crushed at last.

Whilst Han Solo led the strike team against the Imperial shield generator, General Calrissian and Nien Nunb fronted the attack on the second Death Star. Lando flew the *Millennium Falcon* at the head of the Alliance Fleet.

The Ewoks used their cunning to lay traps for the Imperial biker scouts on Endor. Paploo stole a speeder bike to provide a distraction for the Rebels.

IDENTITY FILE

The Ewoks were a tree-dwelling species native to the forest moon of Endor. They were completely covered in fur and had large, mirror-like eyes. Each Ewok village was ruled by a Council of Elders, at the head of which was the Chief. The Ewoks had a deep sense of spirituality that stemmed from their belief that they were all descendants of the Great Tree, a sacred tree in the forest.

They lived high above the forest floor in an intricate network of platforms and huts amongst the treetops. They used primitive stone-level weapons and were hunter-gatherers by nature, living off plants, berries and animals. They were also skilled in the use of bows and catapults, and they hunted in packs to capture large animals.

Because they were small in stature, the Ewoks had to rely on cunning to survive in the forest environment. Setting traps for their prey and developing their weapons for the hunt meant that they were highly skilled in forest survival. Although they lacked an advanced technological culture, they were quick learners. They soon adapted their hunting techniques to fight the Imperial forces based on their world.

UNWANTED VISITORS

After the destruction of the first Death Star, the Emperor built a second, more powerful Death Star in the Outer Rim territories above the moon of Endor. The location was perfect; it was remote and the Endor moon had the right atmosphere to sustain human life. Darth Vader himself was overseeing the final stages of its construction.

To protect the battle station during its construction, a ground force was sent down to the surface of the moon to build a shield generator. These Imperial troops thought that the Ewoks were too primitive a race to be a threat. They set up base near Bright Tree Village. The visitors were regarded with much suspicion and a young scout called Wicket observed their movements very closely.

Luke Skywalker, Han Solo, Chewbacca, C-3PO and R2-D2 landed on Endor to locate the shield generator and destroy it. However, they were captured by an Ewok trap and were taken back to the village. On seeing the shimmering golden colour of C-3PO, the Ewoks believed him to be a god, and set about preparing the other Rebels as a sacrifice to him.

CHIEF CHIRPA

Chief Chirpa was the leader of the tribe of Ewoks at Bright Tree Village. He was grey-furred and carried a totem made of reptile bone. On his head he wore a crown of leaves adorned with the teeth and horns of animals he had hunted.

After capturing the Rebels he was impressed by their good nature and by the storytelling of C-3PO. He agreed to include them as part of the tribe and to help them on their mission to destroy the Imperial shield generator.

It was his decision to involve the Ewoks in the battle on Endor. They lost many lives but ultimately were victorious in bringing down the Imperial shield generator. This allowed the Rebel fleet to attack and destroy the Death Star in orbit above the moon.

Although their technology was primitive, the Ewoks were highly skilled craftspeople and fashioned stone tools for hunting, catapults and simple traps.

WICKET

Wicket W. Warrick was a brave and valiant warrior who excelled in hunting tactics. He was responsible for many of the tactics in the battle against the Imperial forces on the moon of Endor. After witnessing an AT-ST explode after stumbling over the terrain he quickly made up his mind that the Imperial forces could be defeated.

Wicket befriended the injured Princess Leia when he discovered her unconscious in the forest. Nervous at first, he was won over by her gentle nature and took her back to his village to introduce her to the Council of Elders. It was here that Leia discovered her Rebel friends being prepared as a sacrifice to C-3PO. Once the misunderstanding was cleared up, C-3PO told the Ewoks about the Rebellion and the tribal Council agreed to help them.

In the following battle, Wicket showed great courage. His scouting missions had provided the Ewoks with plenty of ammunition to use against the Imperial troops.

LOGRAY

Logray, the medicine man, was not only a healer but also the spiritual leader of the tribe. He had once been a fierce warrior, but in his later years he served Bright Tree Village with his medicines and potions. He had stripy fur and wore a headdress of feathers and the skull of a large bird. He also carried a totem made from a long backbone of a defeated enemy. Logray was often thought to be as old as the forest itself.